Student Edition

¡Hola!

John De Mado
Linda West Tibensky

Marcela Gerber, Series Consultant

Wright Group

The **McGraw·Hill** Companies

www.WrightGroup.com

 **Wright Group**

Send all inquiries to:
Wright Group/McGraw-Hill
P.O. Box 812960
Chicago, IL 60681

ISBN 0-07-602896-8

11 QDB 11

The **McGraw·Hill** Companies

Contenido

Unidad 1

Unidad 2

Unidad 3

Unidad 4

Unidad 5

Unidad 6

Unidad 7

Unidad 8

Unidad 9

Unidad 10

Student Edition

¡Hola!

¡Bienvenidos!

Objetivos

- To learn how to say hello and good-bye
- To ask people their names and introduce yourself
- To talk about how you feel
- To name different objects and people in your classroom
- To use numbers to do everyday things
- To learn about compound names in Spanish

A group of friends greets one another in Chile.

Two friends catch up before entering the metro in Madrid, Spain.

¿Sabías que...?

¿Sabías que. . . ? means "Did you know . . . ?" Whenever you see **¿Sabías que. . . ?** look for interesting facts about the Spanish-speaking world, including how it affects our lives. For instance,

• Colorado and Florida are words that come from Spanish. **Colorado** means "red" (for the red rock common in that state), and **Florida** means "full of flowers."

• There are more than 30 million Spanish speakers in the United States. This means that the United States has the fourth largest Spanish-speaking population in the world!

• Tortilla chips and salsa, which originally come from Mexico, are now a very popular snack food in the United States.

¿Cómo se dice?

What's your name?

Why not choose a Spanish name for yourself? It can be the Spanish version of your name, if there is one, or a brand new name that you like. You can use it during Spanish class—and afterward. There is a list of names on pages 248–249 of this book. Your teacher may have some suggestions, too.

¡Úsalo!

Some boys and girls are waiting to meet with you after school. Look at their names and faces. Then answer the questions on a sheet of paper.

MODELO ¿Cómo se llama el chico?

Se llama Ernesto.

1. ¿Cómo se llama la chica?

2. ¿Cómo se llama el chico?

3. ¿Cómo se llama la chica?

4. ¿Cómo se llama la chica?

5. ¿Cómo se llama el chico?

6. ¿Cómo te llamas?

CONEXIÓN CON LA CULTURA

Compound Names It is customary in many Spanish-speaking countries to have a two-part first name. For example, María Cristina, María del Carmen, and María Isabel are all common names. Boys often have compound names, too, such as José Luis, José Miguel, and Pedro Javier. What are some compound names in English?

Entre amigos

Entre amigos means "among friends." These fun activities let you use Spanish to talk with your classmates. Here's a good example:

Write your name on four index cards. Put the cards in a box with your classmates' cards. Mix them up, then have everyone draw four cards. (If you draw a card with your own name, put it back and take a new one.)

Walk around the classroom asking **¿Cómo te llamas?** so the four classmates whose cards you have can say their names. Return each card after you match it. The first student to return all four cards is the winner.

Compara

En inglés	En español
Mrs. Rodriguez	la Sra. Rodríguez (señora)
Miss Fuentes	la Srta. Fuentes (señorita)
Mr. López	el Sr. López (señor)

En resumen

¿Cómo **te llamas?**
   Me llamo Teresa.

¿Cómo **se llama** el chico?
   Se llama Ernesto.

¿Cómo **se llama** la chica?
   Se llama Rosa.

¿Cómo se dice?

Hello and good-bye

How are you?

¡Úsalo!

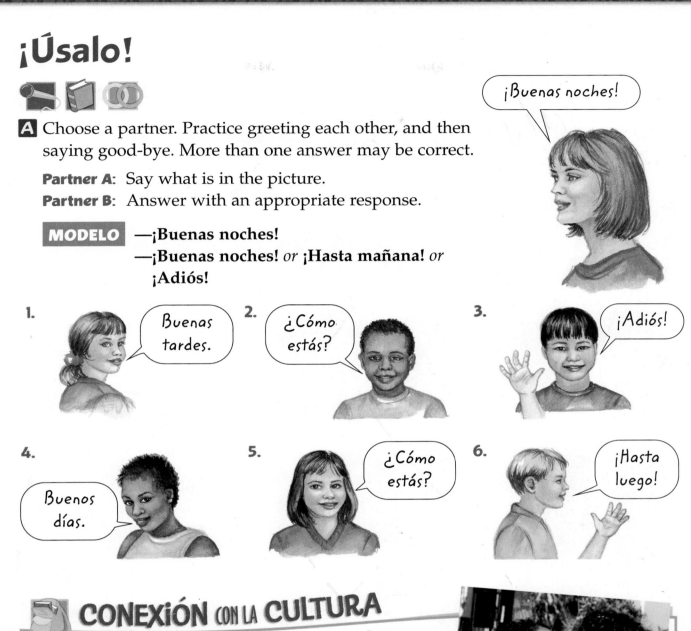

A Choose a partner. Practice greeting each other, and then saying good-bye. More than one answer may be correct.

Partner A: Say what is in the picture.

Partner B: Answer with an appropriate response.

> **MODELO** —¡Buenas noches!
> —¡Buenas noches! *or* ¡Hasta mañana! *or*
> ¡Adiós!

¡Buenas noches!

1. Buenas tardes.

2. ¿Cómo estás?

3. ¡Adiós!

4. Buenos días.

5. ¿Cómo estás?

6. ¡Hasta luego!

CONEXIÓN CON LA CULTURA

Greetings In Spanish-speaking countries, it is common to greet friends and acquaintances by kissing them on the cheek—or once on each cheek in some places. People of all ages greet each other this way. In more formal situations, adults shake hands. How do you greet your friends? How do you greet your parents' or guardians' friends? How do your parents' and or guardians' friends greet each other?

B How do your new friends feel? Work with a partner. Look at the pictures and take the part of the friend as you answer your partner's questions. Then switch roles.

MODELO —¿Cómo estás, Ernesto?

—**Estoy muy mal.** *or* **Muy mal.**

1. ¿Cómo estás, Rosa?

2. ¿Cómo estás, José?

3. ¿Cómo estás, Ana?

4. ¿Cómo estás, Isabel?

5. ¿Cómo estás, Carlos?

En resumen

Hola.
Buenos días.
Buenas tardes.
Buenas noches.
¿Cómo estás?
¿Qué tal?
    Muy bien, gracias.
    Bien, bien.
    Más o menos.
    Así, así.
    Estoy muy mal.

Adiós.
Hasta pronto.
Hasta luego.
Hasta mañana.

¡Bienvenidos!

¿Cómo se dice?

What's this?

¡Úsalo!

Work with a partner. Sketch a classroom object. Show it to your partner and ask him or her what it is. Your partner has to give the correct answer. Switch roles until you have drawn and identified all the classroom objects you know in Spanish.

Partner A: Sketch an object and ask your partner what it is.

Partner B: Say what the object is.

MODELO —¿Qué es?

—Es la silla.

Entre amigos

Get together in a group of three or four classmates. Create labels for everything you know in Spanish in your own classroom. One person reads the name of the object written on a label, for example **la puerta.** Someone else volunteers to go and place the label on the correct object. When that person approaches the object, he or she stops and asks the rest of the group, pointing to the door in this case: **¿Qué es?** The rest of the group has to agree and say **Es la puerta.** before the volunteer can place the label on it.

En resumen

¿Qué es?	¿Qué es?
Es el escritorio.	**Es** la computadora.
el pizarrón.	la luz.
el pupitre.	la puerta.
	la silla.

¿Cómo se dice?

Who is it?

¿Quién es?

Es el maestro.

el maestro
El maestro es un hombre.

¿Cómo estás?

la maestra
La maestra es una mujer.

el alumno
El alumno es un chico.

la alumna
La alumna es una chica.

¡Úsalo!

A Get together with a partner. Ask and answer each other's questions about these people.

Partner A: Ask the question.

Partner B: Look at the picture and answer.

> **MODELO** —¿Quién es?
>
> —Es el alumno.

1.

2.

3.

4.

Now ask each other the same question about different people in your classroom!

B Play a guessing game with a partner. Think of a classroom object and pretend that you're using it. Your partner has to guess what the object is and ask you about it.

Partner A: Pretend you're using the object—for instance, that you're opening a door.

Partner B: Guess what your partner is using and ask your partner.

Partner A: Tell your partner what you are using.

> **MODELO** —¿Es la puerta?
>
> —Sí, es la puerta. *or* No. Es el pizarrón.

C Work with a partner. Ask and answer each other's questions about the picture using **¿Qué es?** or **¿Quién es?** Together, make a list of the people and things you see.

Entre amigos

Bring photographs of your friends and family to class, or cut out pictures from magazines and give the people in them names. Now get together with a partner. Show him or her your pictures. Your partner will point to the people in each picture and ask **¿Quién es?** You should answer **Es (Juan).** Your partner writes the people's names underneath the pictures. Then ask about your partner's pictures and write down the names you hear. Use the list of names in the back of your book for help with spelling.

En resumen

¿Quién **es?**	¿Quién **es?**
Es el alumno.	**Es** la alumna.
el chico.	la chica.
el hombre.	la mujer.
el maestro.	la maestra.

16   dieciséis

¡Bienvenidos!

¿Cómo se dice?

Numbers from 1 to 10

—¿Cuál es el número?
—Es el siete.

0 cero
1 uno
2 dos
3 tres
4 cuatro
5 cinco
6 seis
7 siete
8 ocho
9 nueve
10 diez

¿Sabías que...?

Baseball is a very popular sport in all of the Caribbean region. This is why there are many famous baseball players in the United States from Cuba, the Dominican Republic, and Puerto Rico, as well as from Panama and Venezuela. Locate the Caribbean Sea on a map and name some of the other countries in this region.

Numbers from 11 to 20

—¿Es el doce?
—No, es el diecisiete.

11 once

12 doce

13 trece

14 catorce

15 quince

16 dieciséis

17 diecisiete

18 dieciocho

19 diecinueve

20 veinte

Numbers from 21 to 29

—¿Qué número es?
—Es el veinticuatro.

21 veintiuno

22 veintidós

23 veintitrés

24 veinticuatro

25 veinticinco

26 veintiséis

27 veintisiete

28 veintiocho

29 veintinueve

¡Úsalo!

CONEXIÓN CON LAS MATEMÁTICAS

Making Bar Graphs Work with a partner to make a tally of the students in your class or group. Count the students and tell your partner how many there are. Your partner writes down this number. Then your partner counts the number of girls and the number of boys, and tells you so that you can write these numbers down.

Together, make a bar graph of the number of boys and girls in the classroom. If possible, count the students in other classrooms to make more graphs. Write down what fraction of each classroom is made up of boys and what fraction is made up of girls.

¿Sabías que...?

Spanish speakers often write the number seven (7) like this (7), to make it look different from one (1). And in many Spanish-speaking countries, amounts of money and other numbers are written with commas instead of periods, and periods instead of commas. Seven thousand dollars would be written as $7.000,00 or 7.000,00 $.

En resumen

¿Cuál es el número?
Es el siete. (7)

¿Es el doce? (12)
No, es el diecisiete. (17)

¿Qué número es?
Es el veinticuatro. (24)

¿Cómo se dice?

All kinds of numbers

¡Úsalo!

A If you could make up your own phone number, what would it be? With a partner, create a phone directory of the students in your class. Write down the names of all your classmates. Divide up the class with your partner to survey everyone, asking for their made-up phone numbers. Write the numbers on your list.

> **MODELO** —¿Cuál es tu número de teléfono?
>
> —Es el cinco, seis, seis, uno, nueve, ocho, ocho.

Now ask your partner for the phone numbers you did not write down. Tell your partner the numbers he or she does not have. Work together to complete the class phone directory.

Partner A: Ask for the made-up phone number of the person listed.

Partner B: Say the phone number.

> **MODELO** —¿Cuál es el número de teléfono de Ana?
>
> —Es el ocho, dos, cuatro, siete, cuatro, tres, dos.

Business phone book from Medellín, Colombia

B Write down ten addition problems using numbers less than ten. Say each probem in Spanish to your partner, who writes it down and solves it. Then your partner tells you the answer, and you write it down on your sheet of paper. Alternate with your partner to solve his or her math problems.

Partner A: Write a problem and read it to your partner.

Partner B: Solve the problem and say the answer.

> MODELO —¿Cuánto es cuatro más seis?
>
> —Cuatro más seis es diez.

CONEXIÓN CON LA SALUD

Emergency Phone Numbers Work with a group of classmates to create a list of emergency phone numbers for your home. First, decide which are the most important numbers. These might include a parent's or guardian's work number, the police, the fire department, the poison control center, an ambulance service, the hospital, and 911.

Then create a symbol for each one. Take turns writing those numbers you know and looking for other numbers in the phone book. One person reads out the number in Spanish and everyone else writes it down on his or her list. Bring the list home to post near the phone or on the refrigerator in case of emergency.

En resumen

¿Cuál es tu número de teléfono?
   Es el cuatro, dos, seis, ocho, uno, dos, dos.
   (426–8122)

¿Cuánto es diez más seis? (10 + 6)
   Diez más seis es dieciséis.
   (10 + 6 = 16)

El salón de clase

Colonial-style school in La Serena, Chile

Objetivos

- To name classroom objects and school supplies
- To talk about people or things
- To ask about what people have
- To learn about schools and classrooms in Spanish-speaking countries
- To compare flags of different countries

Children at school in
Tiwanaku, Bolivia

An Ecuadorian
classroom

¿Sabías que...?

- In many schools in Spain and Latin America, students wear uniforms.

- In most schools in Spanish-speaking countries, students buy their own books—even in public schools.

- Some schools in Spain and Latin America are very old. **El Colegio Mayor de Nuestra Señora del Rosario** in Bogotá, Colombia, is more than 250 years old.

¿Cómo se dice?

What is it?

el salón de clase

—¿Qué es?

—Es el salón de clase.

la bandera

la ventana

el reloj

la pared

el mapa

el marcador

la tiza

el borrador

la mesa

el globo

la papelera

Spanish Geography Words

Spanish Geography Words The Spanish word **mesa** is also an English word. In English, a *mesa* is a high, rocky hill with a flat top. There are many mesas in the southwestern United States, such as those in Mesa, Arizona. Why do you think this landform is called a *mesa?* Many places in the southwestern United States have Spanish names because they were settled by people from Spain. What streets or places in your community or state have Spanish names?

¡Úsalo!

Work with a partner to name different classroom objects in Spanish. Choose one of the objects pictured below. On a sheet of paper, draw a blank space for each letter in its name. Write in one of the letters. Show the sheet to your partner and ask him or her what the object is. Your partner guesses the object you're thinking of and writes its complete name. Then switch roles with your partner.

Partner A: Write blanks for each letter in the name of an object.

Partner B: Guess what classroom object it is, based on the blanks.

MODELO —¿Qué es?

—Es el globo.

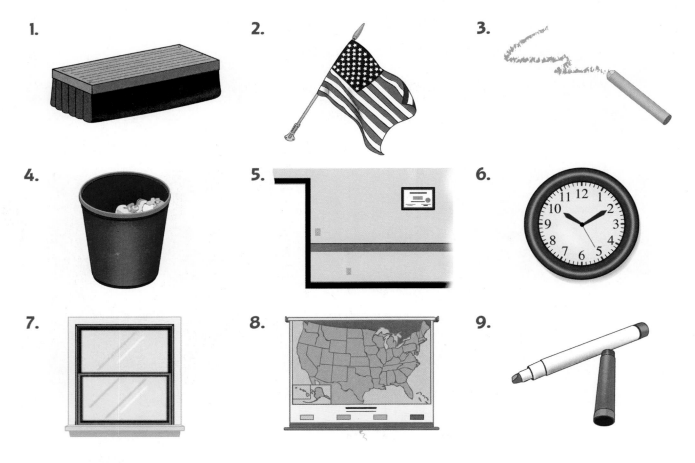

1.

2.

3.

4.

5.

6.

7.

8.

9.

Entre amigos

Are you good at matching up words and pictures?

Work with a partner. Partner A writes the names of five classroom objects on index cards. Partner B draws each of the objects Partner A wrote on separate index cards.

Partner A chooses a word card while Partner B chooses a drawing card. Do not show them to each other. Partner A reads the word and uses it to ask Partner B if it matches his or her drawing:

¿Es la bandera?

Partner B looks at his or her drawing and answers:

Sí, es la bandera.
or
No, no es la bandera. Es el mapa.

Set aside the names and drawings that match. Continue until you have matched all drawings with their names.

En resumen

¿Qué es?

Es el borrador.	Es la bandera
el globo.	la mesa.
el mapa.	la papelera.
el marcador.	la pared.
el reloj.	la tiza.
el salón de clase.	la ventana.

¿Cómo se dice?

What's on the desk?

—¿Qué hay en el pupitre?

—Hay un cuaderno.

el bolígrafo

el libro

el cuaderno

la hoja de papel

la regla

el lápiz

¿Tienes un libro?

Sí, claro.

¡Úsalo!

A Sketch your desk with three school supplies on it. Then get together with a partner and ask if your partner has the following objects on his or her "desk." Your partner answers according to what he or she drew.

> **MODELO** —¿Tienes un lápiz en el pupitre?
>
> —Sí, claro. *or* No.

2.

3.

4

5.

6.

¿Sabías que...?

In Latin America, many schools are actually two schools in one! One group of students comes in the morning. The other group comes in the afternoon, uses the same classrooms, and leaves in the evening. Even the teachers are different! Why do you think classes share the same rooms?

B You're making a list of school supplies that you need to buy for class. In one column **(Sí),** write supplies that you already have. In another column **(No),** write the supplies that you need to buy. Then get together with a partner and find out what he or she has or doesn't have. Take turns asking each other what you have on your **Sí** lists.

Partner A: Ask if your partner has an object.

Partner B: Check your list and answer the question.

<table>
<tr><td>MODELO</td><td>—¿Tienes una regla?</td></tr>
<tr><td></td><td>—Sí. *or* Sí, claro. *or* No.</td></tr>
</table>

Sí	No
una regla	

Entre amigos

Play a game with the names of all the classroom objects and school supplies you know in Spanish. Everyone in the class will take one index card and write on it the name of an object in the class. For example, **un bolígrafo.**

Your teacher will collect all the cards, shuffle them and put them face down on a table or desk.

Your teacher will divide the class into two teams. Members of each team will take turns picking a card, reading it aloud, and then pointing to the object it describes. If the team member is correct, his or her team gets a point. If the team member is not correct, the other team gets a point.

The first team to get 20 points is the winner.

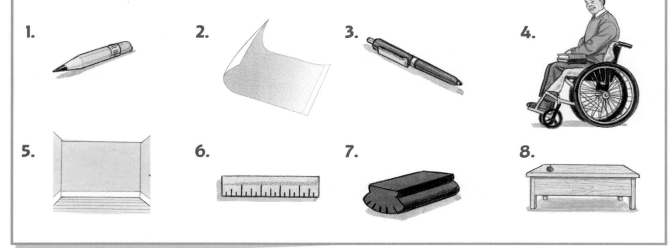

CONEXIÓN CON LAS MATEMÁTICAS

Units of Measurement Look at the pictures and decide if the object shown is best measured in meters or centimeters. Then write the names of the objects in order, from smallest to largest.

1.

2.

3.

4.

5.

6.

7.

8.

¿Sabías que...?

In most countries in Latin America and in many other parts of the world, the metric system of measurement is commonly used. Instead of miles, pounds, and gallons, the measurement units are kilometers, kilograms, and liters. Give examples of the kinds of things that are measured in kilometers, kilograms, and liters.

AREA DE
NEBLINA
PROXIMOS 12 KMS

En resumen

¿Qué **hay** en el pupitre?

Hay un bolígrafo.
    un cuaderno.
    un lápiz.
    un libro.
    una hoja de papel.
    una regla.

¿Cómo se dice?

Talking about more than one

Look at these words. How do they change when there is more than one?

un globo   **dos globos**   **una mesa**   **tres mesas**

In Spanish, words that end in the letters **a, e, i, o,** or **u** add the letter **-s** when you talk about more than one.

Now look at these words. How do they change when there is more than one?

un borrador   **dos borradores**   **un reloj**   **cuatro relojes**

In Spanish, words that *don't* end in **a, e, i, o,** or **u** add the letters **-es** when you talk about more than one.

If you want to ask how many there are of something, you say **¿Cuántos hay?** or **¿Cuántas hay?**

You use **cuántos** with words that use **el / un,** and **cuántas** with words that use **la / una.**

¿Cuántos bolígrafos hay?
Hay dos.
¿Cuántas sillas hay?
Hay veinticuatro.

CONEXIÓN CON LOS ESTUDIOS SOCIALES

Parts of the Globe Look at the map and answer the questions below.

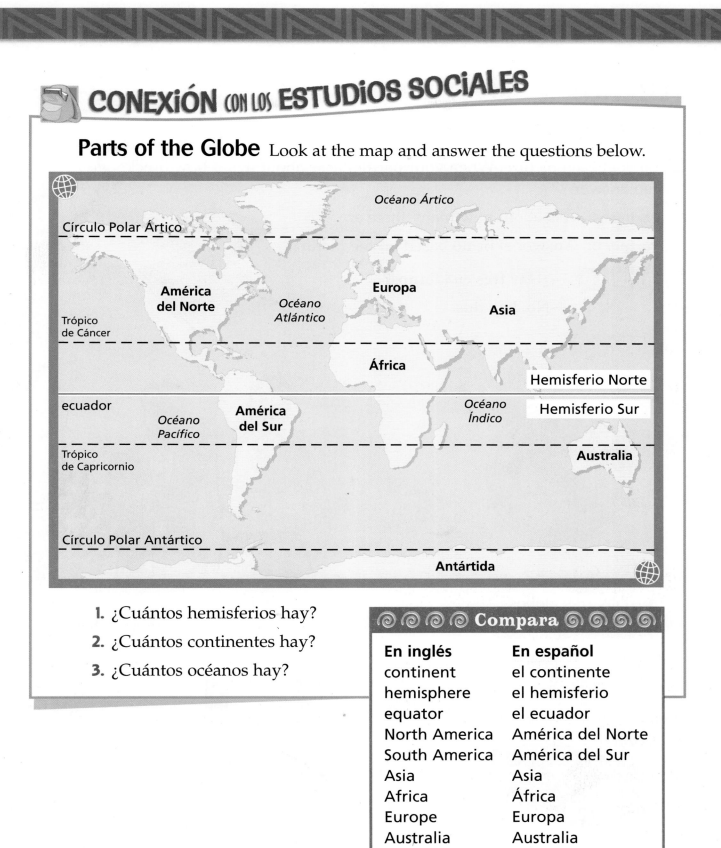

Océano Ártico

Círculo Polar Ártico

América del Norte

Océano Atlántico

Europa

Asia

Trópico de Cáncer

África

Hemisferio Norte

ecuador

Océano Pacífico

América del Sur

Océano Índico

Hemisferio Sur

Trópico de Capricornio

Australia

Círculo Polar Antártico

Antártida

1. ¿Cuántos hemisferios hay?
2. ¿Cuántos continentes hay?
3. ¿Cuántos océanos hay?

◎ ◎ ◎ ◎ **Compara** ◎ ◎ ◎ ◎

En inglés	En español
continent	el continente
hemisphere	el hemisferio
equator	el ecuador
North America	América del Norte
South America	América del Sur
Asia	Asia
Africa	África
Europe	Europa
Australia	Australia
Antarctica	Antártida

¡Úsalo!

A Look at each picture. When your partner asks about it, see how quickly you can answer.

Partner A: Ask about how many there are.

Partner B: Answer **sí** or **no** based on the picture.

MODELO	—¿Hay tres cuadernos?
	—No, hay dos.

1. ¿Hay tres globos?

2. ¿Hay dos maestros?

3. ¿Hay cuatro borradores?

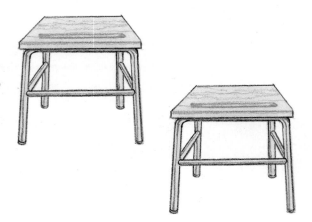

4. ¿Hay dos pupitres?

B For each item, tell how many there are. Write your answers on a sheet of paper.

MODELO **Hay tres relojes.**

1.

2.

3.

4.

5.

6.

C Count things you know in Spanish in your classroom, including the people. Keep a tally of each object and person on a chart like this one. Work with a partner to compare lists. See if your lists match.

MODELO —¿**Cuántos borradores hay?**

—**Hay (seis) borradores.**
or **No hay borradores.**

1. el borrador	✔✔✔✔✔✔	
2. la pared		
3. el alumno		
4. el maestro		
5. la maestra		
6. la silla		
7. la regla		
8. el pupitre		
9. la puerta		
10. la alumna		
11. el globo		
12. el marcador		
13. la ventana		

D These pictures are similar, but there are ten differences between them. Work with a partner to find the differences. Each of you should choose one of the scenes and describe what you see to find the differences.

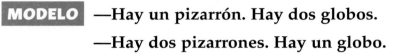 —**Hay un pizarrón. Hay dos globos.**

—**Hay dos pizarrones. Hay un globo.**

CONEXIÓN CON LAS MATEMÁTICAS

Making Pictographs Read the following pictograph. It shows the number of students in each classroom at a school. Read the graph key and tell how many students there are in each classroom.

	Alumnos	Total
Salón 4	☺ ☺ ☺ ☺ ☺	Hay...
Salón 5	☺ ☺ ☺ ☺ ☺ ☺	
Salón 6	☺ ☺ ☺ ☺	
Salón 7	☺ ☺ ☺ ☺ ☺ ☺ ☺	

☺ = 3 alumnos

Now choose several common classroom objects, such as pens, pencils, chairs, and books. Working with a partner, make a pictograph that compares how many of these objects there are in your classroom. Write a sentence for each object that describes how many there are.

En resumen

un globo	dos globos	Cuántos bolígrafos hay?
reloj	relojes	Hay dos.
una mesa	dos mesas	Cuántas sillas hay?
pared	paredes	Hay veinticuatro.

Lección 4

¿Cómo se dice?

Talking about people and things

Look at the examples. Notice how the words **el** and **la** change when you talk about more than one person.

el alumno   **los alumnos**   **la alumna**   **las alumnas**

Notice how **el** and **la** change when you talk about more than one thing.

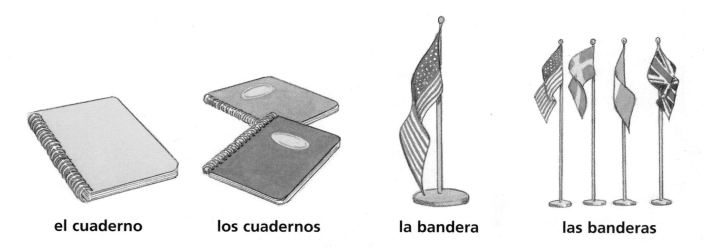

el cuaderno   **los cuadernos**   **la bandera**   **las banderas**

Did you notice that **el** changes to **los** and **la** changes to **las** when you talk about more than one person or thing?

When you want to know what something is, you ask **¿Qué es?** To ask about more than one thing, use the question **¿Qué son?** When you want to know who someone is, you ask **¿Quién es?** and when you want to know who several or many people are, you ask **¿Quiénes son?**

40 cuarenta   Unidad 1

¡Úsalo!

A You're helping your teacher put supplies and furniture in your classroom. Draw a chart like this one on a separate sheet of paper. Write an ✗ next to five kinds of objects you will help bring. Get together with a partner and ask which objects he or she has, and answer your partner's questions.

MODELO —¿Qué tienes?

—Los pupitres y el globo.

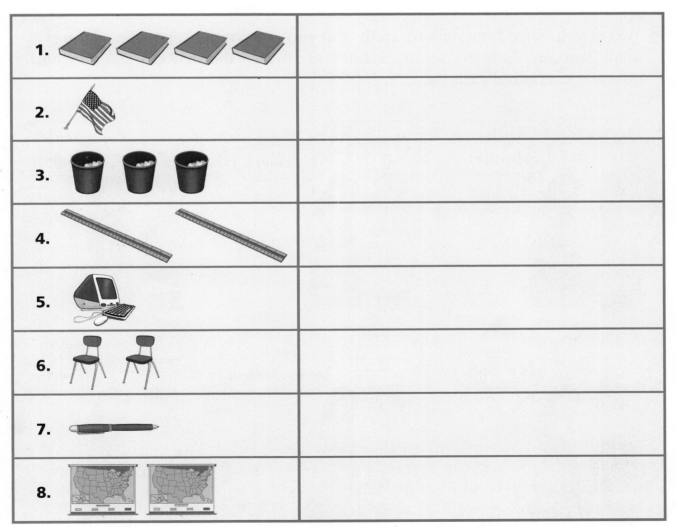

B Write the following responses on index cards and put them all in a box.

> Son los alumnos.

> Es el cuaderno.

> Es la maestra.

> Son las banderas.

Pick out a card and read it to yourself. Then ask your partner the correct question for that answer, so that he or she can guess which card you picked out.

¿Quién es?	¿Qué es?
¿Quiénes son?	¿Qué son?

C Two of your friends are talking softly and you're having a hard time hearing them. You can't hear the questions, but you can hear the answers. Decide what question was asked each time.

1. ¿_____? Son los bolígrafos.

2. ¿_____? Es la mesa.

3. ¿_____? Son los alumnos.

4. ¿_____? Es el lápiz.

5. ¿_____? Son las computadoras.

6. ¿_____? Es la maestra.

CONEXIÓN CON LOS ESTUDIOS SOCIALES

Country Flags Here are the flags of nine Spanish-speaking countries. What similarities and differences can you see among these flags? How are they similar to and different from the flag of the United States?

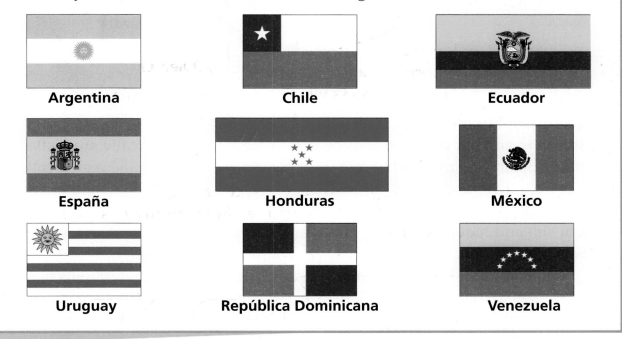

Argentina	Chile	Ecuador
España	Honduras	México
Uruguay	República Dominicana	Venezuela

Entre amigos

Play a guessing game with a partner. Tell your partner to close his or her eyes. Then get an object (or objects) from your desk or from some other place in the room, and have your partner touch it (or them). As your partner is touching the item(s), ask:

¿Qué es? *or* **¿Qué son?**

Your partner has to say the right answer:

Es un lápiz. *or* **Son las tizas.**

Do this with five different items, then switch roles with your partner.

¿Dónde se habla español?

ESPAÑA

Madrid ☆

España

Spain is the second most mountainous country in Europe and its coastlines weave in and out for thousands of miles. Spain's many beaches and generally mild and sunny climate help make tourism an important industry. But sun and mountains aren't all that Spain has to offer.

One of the most important art museums in the world is in Madrid: **el Museo del Prado.** You can see more than 5,000 paintings there! Madrid has been the capital since 1561. Older than Madrid are the caves of Altamira, where there are drawings made by cave dwellers more than 15,000 years

ago. And there really are castles in Spain, mostly in the region called Castilla. Did you know that the word for castle is **el castillo?** You can see a Spanish castle, the Alcazar in Segovia, on the next page.

There are also windmills in Castilla, where the novel *Don Quijote* was set. Have you heard of the adventures of the main character, who mistakes windmills for giants and tries to slay them? Cervantes wrote this story almost 400 years ago. It's still being read today, and it's one of the most translated books in the world.

Spain is the world's leading producer of olive oil. Fishing is also a major industry. The popular Spanish dish, **paella,** is a delicious combination of seafood and rice, seasoned with the world's most expensive spice: saffron. Saffron looks like little pieces of red and orange thread and it comes from a crocus flower. You need 4,000 flowers to make one ounce of saffron!

◎ ◎ ◎ ◎ ◎ Datos ◎ ◎ ◎ ◎ ◎

Capital: Madrid

Ciudades importantes: Barcelona, Bilbao, Sevilla, Valencia

Idiomas oficiales: Español, catalán, vasco, gallego, valenciano

Moneda: El euro

Población: 40.2 millones

Reading Strategy

Using Visuals Before you start to read, look at the pictures on the page. They give you clues about the content. What do you think the reading will be about?

¡Léelo en español!

Los deportes Los españoles practican muchos deportes[1] y el número uno es el fútbol. El fútbol es el deporte más popular. Todas las ciudades importantes tienen[2] un equipo de fútbol. Madrid tiene dos: el Real Madrid y el Atlético de Madrid. El Real Madrid es famoso y muy bueno. Son campeones de Europa. Los españoles también[3] practican el baloncesto, el ciclismo, el golf y el tenis. En el norte de España las personas practican el jai alai.

¡Comprendo!

Choose the correct answers and write them on a sheet of paper.

1. **El catalán** is a _____.
   - **a.** novel
   - **b.** language
   - **c.** sport
   - **d.** celebration

2. **Paella** is a _____.
   - **a.** food
   - **b.** musical group
   - **c.** city
   - **d.** cave

3. Saffron comes from a _____.
   - **a.** seafood
   - **b.** special rice
   - **c.** flower
   - **d.** mountain

4. Spain is a very _____ country.
   - **a.** flat
   - **b.** hilly
   - **c.** cold
   - **d.** mountainous

5. **El castillo** means _____.
   - **a.** windmill
   - **b.** castle
   - **c.** flower
   - **d.** museum

[1] play a lot of sports   [2] have   [3] also

2

Animales de varios colores

A colorful parrot
from Latin America

Objetivos

- To learn the names of colors and shapes
- To identify different animals
- To describe your favorite animals
- To find out about some animals from the Caribbean and South America

A Quechua woman with her baby and llama in Cuzco, Peru

A giant Galapagos tortoise on Isabela Island in Ecuador

¿Sabías que...?

- The largest snake in the world is the South American anaconda. It can grow up to thirty feet long.

- The Galápagos Islands off the coast of Ecuador are home to some of the most unusual animals in the world.

- The black panther of the Central American jungle is really a jaguar whose spots you can't see.

¿Cómo se dice?

What color is it?

—¿De qué color es?

—Es rojo.

rojo

verde

amarillo

anaranjado

rosado

blanco

azul

morado

negro

gris

marrón

¿Sabías que...?

In Spanish, there may be several different ways of saying the same thing. For example, **rojo** is *red*, but another word for *red* is **colorado. Marrón** is *brown*, but in some countries, people say **café.** What other words are there for shades of *red* in English?

What is it?

—¿Qué es?

—Es un triángulo. Es azul.

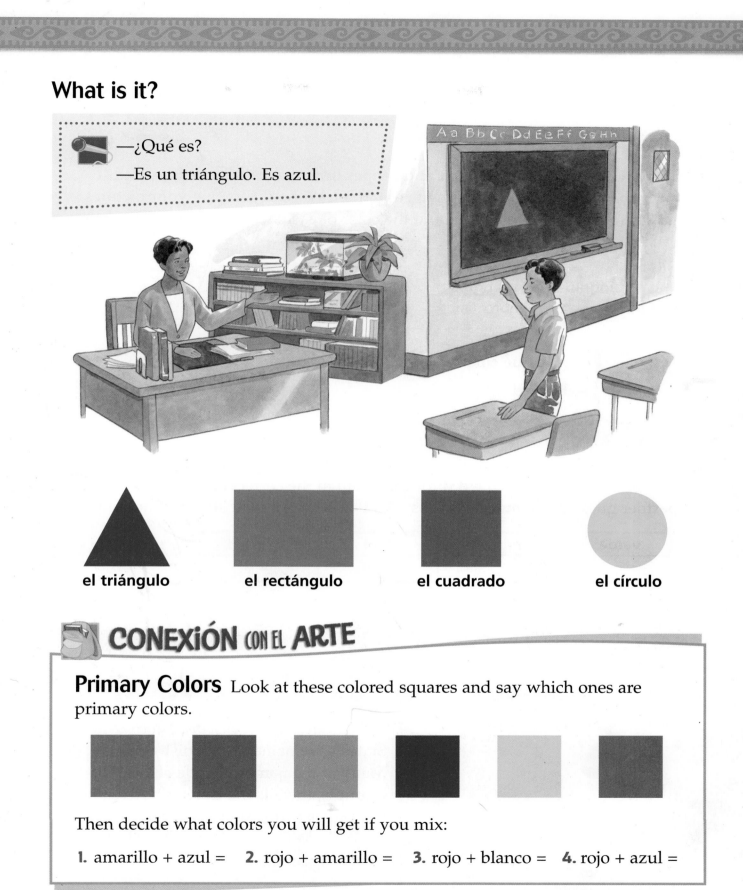

el triángulo   **el rectángulo**   **el cuadrado**   **el círculo**

CONEXIÓN CON EL ARTE

Primary Colors Look at these colored squares and say which ones are primary colors.

Then decide what colors you will get if you mix:

1. amarillo + azul =   **2.** rojo + amarillo =   **3.** rojo + blanco =   **4.** rojo + azul =

¡Úsalo!

A Cut out a picture of these items and shapes from magazines, or draw and color them. Then, get together with a partner. Without showing your pictures, take turns asking each other about the color of each item. Then show them to each other.

el rectángulo	el triángulo	el cuaderno	el círculo
el reloj	el libro	el lápiz	

> **MODELO** —¿De qué color es el marcador?
>
> —Es azul.

B Draw a chart like this one. Then look around your classroom for objects in these colors. Write the Spanish word for each item in the correct column. Have a partner guess the items on your list. Add clues about their shapes if needed.

verde	marrón	azul	gris

Partner A: —Es verde.

Partner B: —¿Es el pizarrón?

Partner A: —No. Es un círculo.

Partner B: —¿Es el reloj?

Partner A: —Sí.

¿Sabías que...?

Many places in the Southwestern United States have names of Spanish origin. Many of the names include colors. For example, there is the Colorado River, the city of Amarillo, Río Blanco county, and Mesa Verde Canyon (remember that a *mesa* is a rocky hill with a flat top).

Entre amigos

Put a puzzle together! Get together with a partner. Gather sheets of construction paper in different colors. Draw and carefully cut out circles, triangles, squares, and rectangles of different sizes from all the sheets of construction paper.

Exchange sheets and cutouts with another pair. Work together with your partner to put the pieces back together.

Partner A: Say the Spanish names of the shapes and colors that are cut out from each sheet.

Partner B: Look for the correct pieces and place them on the sheet.

¿Sabías que...?

There are many expressions in Spanish that use colors to mean something else. For example, **blanco** might be the color of snow, but **el blanco** can also mean target, goal, blank space, or gap.

Here are some others:

al rojo vivo = very hot or very tense

verlo todo de color de rosa = to always look on the bright side

quedarse en blanco = to draw a blank (when trying to remember something)

What are some expressions or phrases in English that use colors?

CONEXIÓN CON LAS MATEMÁTICAS

Perimeter Find the perimeters of these shapes. Then match each perimeter with the correct shape. Check your answers with your partner by telling him or her the shape and color. (Note: Shapes are not drawn to scale.)

MODELO —El número 1 es el triángulo verde.

1. 12 m + 12 m + 15 m =

2. 5 m + 5 m + 5 m + 5 m =

3. 90 cm + 90 cm + 35 cm + 35 cm =

4. 3 m + 9 m + 12 m =

5. 15 cm + 15 cm + 35 cm + 35 cm =

6. 7 m + 7 m + 7 m + 7 m =

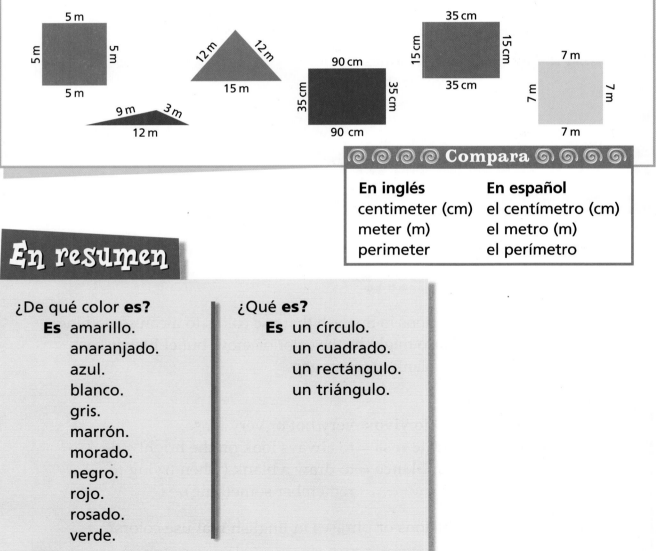

@ @ @ @ **Compara** @ @ @ @

En inglés	En español
centimeter (cm)	el centímetro (cm)
meter (m)	el metro (m)
perimeter	el perímetro

En resumen

¿De qué color **es**?	¿Qué **es**?
Es amarillo.	**Es** un círculo.
anaranjado.	un cuadrado.
azul.	un rectángulo.
blanco.	un triángulo.
gris.	
marrón.	
morado.	
negro.	
rojo.	
rosado.	
verde.	

¿Cómo se dice?

What animal is it?

—¿Qué animal es?

—Es un gato.

—¿De qué color es?

—Es blanco.

el gato   **el pájaro**   **el canario**   **el loro**   **el tigre**

el ratón   **la mariposa**   **el flamenco**   **el conejo**

What's your favorite animal?

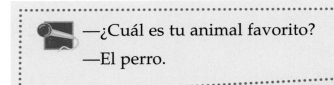

—¿Cuál es tu animal favorito?

—El perro.

el perro

el pez

el oso

◎ ◎ ◎ Compara ◎ ◎ ◎

En inglés	En español
animal	el animal
favorite	favorito

CONEXIÓN CON LAS CIENCIAS

Quetzal The **quetzal** is a beautiful bird found in rain forests from southern Mexico to Costa Rica. It has brilliant colors and a very long tail, which is about two feet long. The Aztecs and Mayas in Central America used the bird's feathers in their ceremonies. The **quetzal** is the national bird of Guatemala, where the coins and bills are also called **quetzales.** How would you describe in Spanish the colors of the **quetzal?**

¡Úsalo!

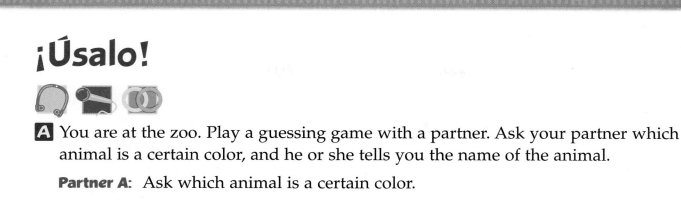

A You are at the zoo. Play a guessing game with a partner. Ask your partner which animal is a certain color, and he or she tells you the name of the animal.

Partner A: Ask which animal is a certain color.

Partner B: Find the animal in the picture and answer.

> **MODELO** —¿Qué animal es azul?
>
> —El flamenco.

¿Sabías que...?

Flamingos are pink because of the shrimp they eat. They are a perfect example of the saying, *You are what you eat!* Chemicals inside the shrimp turn feathers a reddish color. The colors of flamingos range from dark red to bright pink. Flamingos can be found in many places in South America, including Peru, Argentina, Chile, Bolivia, Uruguay, and Paraguay.

B Play a game with a partner. Together, draw a gameboard like this one. Draw an animal you know in each square.

On each of several small index cards, write the numbers 1, 2, or 3. Put them facedown in a pile. You'll also need two coins or buttons for markers.

You're ready to play! Draw a number card. If you draw a 2, for example, move forward two squares. When you land on a square, your partner asks **¿Qué animal es? ¿De qué color es?** If you give the correct answers, you can keep your spot. If you're wrong, you have to go back to where you were.

Take turns drawing numbers. The first one to get to the finish line wins the game!

CONEXIÓN CON LAS CIENCIAS

Biodiversity Costa Rica is well known for its *biodiversity*, or the different types of plants and animals that live there. About one quarter of the country's land is protected. Hundreds of species of mammals, birds, amphibians, and reptiles live in Costa Rica.

En resumen

¿Qué animal **es**? ¿Cuál **es** tu animal favorito?	**Es** el canario. el conejo. el flamenco. el gato. el loro. el oso.	el pájaro. el perro. el pez. el ratón. el tigre. la mariposa.

¿Cómo se dice?

Describing things

Colors are one way to describe things. Look at these sentences to see how to say that different things are yellow.

El canario es amarill**o**.   **La** mariposa es amarill**a**.   **La** luz es amarill**a**.

Did you notice that sometimes the word is **amarillo** and sometimes it's **amarilla?** Many descriptive words end in **-o** or **-a** (like **amarillo** and **amarilla**). These descriptive words end in **-o** with words that use **el.** They end in **-a** with words that use **la.**

Some descriptive words don't end in **-o** or **-a.** Look at these sentences. Notice how the descriptive word is used.

El loro es **verde.**   **La** pared es **verde.**

Did you see that the descriptive word is the same in both cases? Descriptive words that don't end in **-o** or **-a** stay the same for words that use **el** and words that use **la.**

Now, here are some words you can use to talk about sizes and shapes: If you want to ask for a description of something, ask **¿Cómo es?**

—¿Cómo es el perro?
—Es flaco.

grande

pequeño

|←——— largo ———→| |← corto →|

flaco

gordo

¡Úsalo!

A Read each sentence and complete it with the correct word. Then draw and color each item on a separate sheet of paper.

> **MODELO** El bolígrafo es (rosado, rosada).
>
> El bolígrafo es rosado.

1. La mariposa es (rojo, roja).
2. La pared es (blanco, blanca).
3. El tigre es (anaranjado, anaranjada).
4. El oso es (negro, negra).
5. La regla es (morado, morada).
6. El mapa es (amarillo, amarilla).

B With your partner, make a catalog for the school store. Your partner suggests items and you ask what they are like. Then you draw them on a sheet of paper and label them. Switch roles after completing each page.

Partner A: Say the name of an object.

Partner B: Ask what color the object should be and what it is like.

Partner A: Say the color and describe the object.

Partner B: Draw, color, and label the object.

Compara

En inglés	En español
mammals	los mamíferos
manatee	el manatí

CONEXIÓN CON LAS CIENCIAS

Manatees Manatees are mammals that live in warm fresh water and salt water around Florida, the Caribbean, South America, and West Africa. Manatees can grow to 15 feet (4.5 meters) and weigh 1,500 pounds (680 kilograms). Like humans, manatees are mammals. They give birth to calves in the water. How would you describe the manatee in Spanish?

C Make a chart like this one. Look around the classroom and write the names of objects you see under the correct description. Then tell a partner about the objects you included in your chart.

MODELO La tiza es corta.

grande	largo/larga	corto/corta	pequeño/pequeña
		la tiza	

Entre amigos

Bring in a picture of your favorite animal. Get together with three or four classmates and show your picture. The people in your group will ask you different questions, such as **¿Cuál es tu animal favorito?, ¿Cómo se llama?, ¿De qué color es?,** and **¿Cómo es?** After they're done, you can add any information they might have missed.

Here are the names of some other animals:

| horse | **el caballo** | duck | **el pato** | donkey | **el burro** |
| cow | **la vaca** | hen | **la gallina** | | |

En resumen

El canario es amarill**o**.
La mariposa es amarill**a**.

El loro es **verde**.
La pared es **verde**.

¿Cómo **es**?
Es grande.
    pequeño/pequeña.
    largo/larga.
    corto/corta.
    gordo/gorda.
    flaco/flaca.

¿Cómo se dice?

Describing more than one

Look at these sentences. Notice how the words that describe the animals change when we talk about more than one.

El os**o** es negr**o**.

Los os**os** son negr**os**.

La mariposa**a** es amarill**a**.

Las maripos**as** son amarill**as**.

El perr**o** es grand**e**.

Los perr**os** son grand**es**.

If the descriptive word ends in a vowel, then add an **-s** when you talk about more than one. Some descriptive words—for example, **azul**—don't end in a vowel. Add **-es** to these words to talk about more than one.

CONEXIÓN CON LAS CIENCIAS

Camouflage Many species blend in, or *camouflage*, with their surroundings. Camouflage lets creatures hide from their enemies, and also lets predators sneak up on their prey. Some camouflage is a mix of dark and light colors, like the stripes on tigers and zebras.

Look at these pictures of animals that use camouflage. Complete their descriptions with the right colors.

El camaleón es _____ y _____.

El tigre es _____ y _____.

La culebra es _____.

El oso es _____.

⊚ ⊚ ⊚ Compara ⊚ ⊚ ⊚

En inglés	En español
camouflage	el camuflaje
chameleon	el camaleón
zebra	la cebra

¡Úsalo!

A Read each sentence and complete it with the correct word. Then match the pictures with the descriptions.

1. Los canarios son (amarillo, amarillos).
2. La mariposa es (marrón, marrones).
3. Los conejos son (gris, grises).
4. El oso es (negro, negros).
5. Los perros son (blanco, blancos).
6. El flamenco es (rosado, rosados).

a.   b.   c.

d.   e.   f.

B Look at this picture and describe it to a partner. Tell your partner the different objects in the room and describe them. Your partner will make a list of all the objects you talk about.

CONEXIÓN CON LAS MATEMÁTICAS

Making Charts with Data Look at each picture. With a partner, take turns saying how many animals there are and describing their size and color. Work together to copy and complete a chart like this one with your data.

MODELO —Hay cinco osos. Los osos son pequeños. Son marrones.

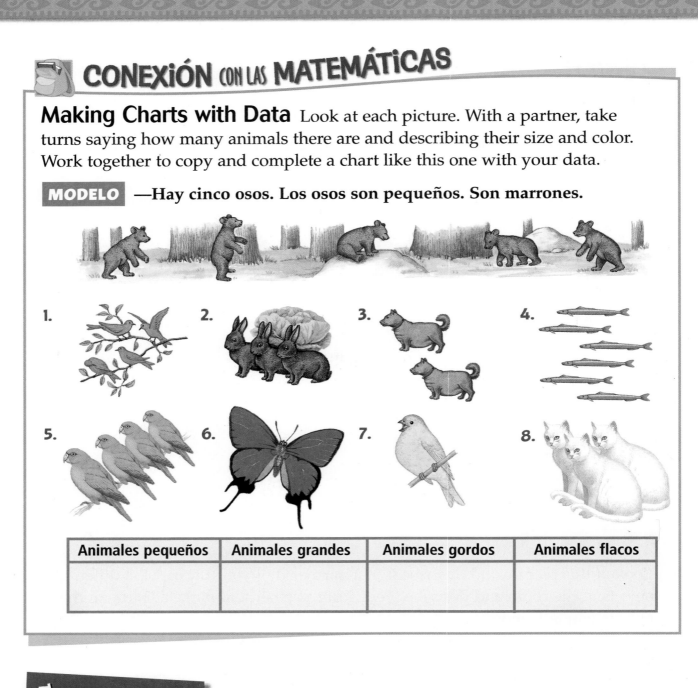

Animales pequeños	Animales grandes	Animales gordos	Animales flacos

En resumen

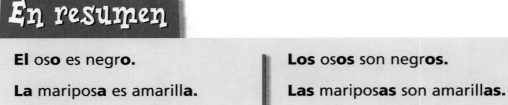

El os**o** es negr**o**.	**Los** os**os** son negr**os**.
La maripos**a** es amarill**a**.	**Las** maripos**as** son amarill**as**.
El perr**o** es grand**e**.	**Los** perr**os** son grand**es**.

¿Cómo se dice?

Talking about things in general

So far you've learned how to use **el** and **la,** as well as **un** and **una.** Do you know when to use one and when to use the other? Look at these examples.

Es **un** gato.   **El** gato es gris.   Es **una** regla.   **La** regla es larga.

You use **un** or **una** to talk about something in general, such as *any* cat, and **el** or **la** to talk about one specific thing, such as a *particular* cat. The English words *a, an,* and *the* work the same way.

Now look at what happens to **un** and **una** when you're talking about more than one thing.

  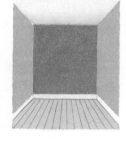

un pez   **unos** peces   **una** pared   **unas** paredes

Un changes to **unos** and **una** changes to **unas.**

¡Úsalo!

A Get together with a partner. Your partner looks at the pictures below and secretly selects one. Then ask him or her **¿Qué es o qué son?** Your partner answers. Keep asking questions about the item until you guess the picture. Then switch roles.

> **MODELO**
> —¿Qué es?
> —Es un oso.
>
> —¿Cómo es el oso?
> —Es grande.
>
> —¿Es blanco?
> —No, es negro.

CONEXIÓN CON LAS CIENCIAS

Coquí Frog The **coquí,** a small frog, lives in Puerto Rico. Like all frogs, it is an amphibian, and it is about the size of a thumbnail. The **coquí** gets its name from the sound it makes: **coquí, coquí, coquí.** You wouldn't believe such a small animal could make so much noise! How do you think the **coquí** frog compares to other frogs you know?

Compara

En inglés	En español
amphibian	anfibio

B Describe this picture to a partner. Say the shape, size, color, and number of things. Your partner makes a drawing based on your description.

Your partner can ask questions such as **¿Qué es?** or **¿Qué son?,** **¿Cómo es?** or **¿Cómo son?, ¿De qué color es?** or **¿De qué colores son?** Then switch roles.

Put your drawings side by side and compare them with the original picture. Point out any differences.

CONEXIÓN CON LAS CIENCIAS

Butterfly Migration Many animals *migrate,* or travel great distances. One of the smallest and most studied migrant animals in the world is the Monarch butterfly. It spends the summer in North America and flies south to the mountains of central Mexico for the winter. The butterflies lay their eggs on the way back north, starting a new life cycle.

With a group, create a poster of the life cycle of the Monarch butterfly. Help each other by describing in Spanish the color and size of each stage so you'll know how to draw each one. Color them and label in Spanish each stage of the life cycle.

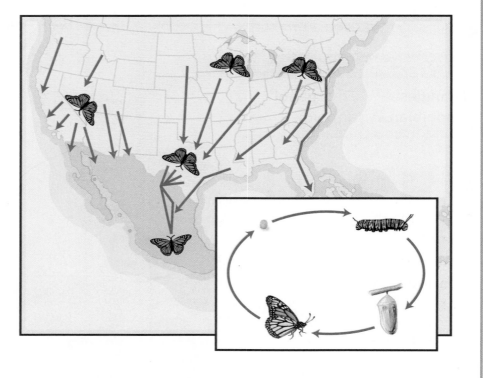

<table>
<tr><th colspan="2">◎ ◎ ◎ Compara ◎ ◎ ◎</th></tr>
<tr><th>En inglés</th><th>En español</th></tr>
<tr><td>adult</td><td>la adulta</td></tr>
<tr><td>cycle</td><td>el ciclo</td></tr>
<tr><td>egg</td><td>el huevo</td></tr>
<tr><td>larva</td><td>la larva</td></tr>
<tr><td>pupa</td><td>la pupa</td></tr>
</table>

Entre amigos

Together with three or four classmates, write in Spanish the names of all the animals you learned about in this unit on separate index cards. Then put them in a small bag.

Pick out one of the cards and imitate the animal named on it. Your classmates will guess the animal (in Spanish, of course), and add a sentence describing the animal. The first person to guess correctly wins a point, and so does the first person who describes the animal correctly! Take turns playing until a person has won eight points.

MODELO   **Es un oso. El oso es blanco. ¡El oso es grande!**

To liven up the game, add Spanish sound effects to your acting.

guau, guau   **miau, miau**   **cua, cua**   **i–o, i–o**

En resumen

Es **un** gato.	**un** pez
El gato es gris.	**unos** pec**es**
Es **una** regla.	**una** pared
La regla es larg**a**.	**unas** pared**es**

¿Dónde se habla español?

México

With a population of more than 21 million in its greater metropolitan area, Mexico City (pictured on the next page) is the third largest city in the world. It was built on the site of the Aztec capital, Tenochtitlan, which had a population of more than 100,000 when the Spaniards arrived in 1519. At that time, very few European cities had such a large population. Legend has it that the Aztecs were told to build their capital on the spot where they'd see an eagle devouring a snake. This image appears on the national flag. The Aztec culture prospered during the 1400s, but even before then, Mexico's indigenous populations had developed advanced and powerful cultures. Today most of Mexico's population is **mestizo,** a blend of these indigenous cultures with the Spaniards, who ruled this land until 1821.

@@@@ @@@@ **Datos** @@@@ @@@@

Capital: México, Distrito Federal

Ciudades importantes: Acapulco, Cuernavaca, Guadalajara, Monterrey, Puebla, Veracruz

Idiomas: Español y lenguas indígenas

Moneda: El peso mexicano

Población: 104.9 millones

¡Léelo en español!

Los mariachis La música de los mariachis es muy popular en todo el mundo.[1] Los mariachis son grupos pequeños o grandes que tocan[2] instrumentos musicales y cantan[3] canciones tradicionales. Los mariachis tocan guitarras y trompetas. Tocan música en los restaurantes y en las casas[4] para celebrar ocasiones especiales. Llevan[5] ropa tradicional: los trajes[6] son negros y las camisas son blancas y muy elegantes.

[1] all over the world   [2] (they) play   [3] they sing
[4] homes   [5] They wear   [6] suits

Using Cognates Before you begin reading, look at the selection and see how many words look like words you know in English. Words that look the same in English and Spanish usually mean the same thing. They are called cognates. But be careful of false cognates! What do you think **ropa** means? Read the selection to check your answer.

¡Comprendo!

The following statements are false. Rewrite them to make them true. Write your answers on a sheet of paper.

1. Most of Mexico's population is indigenous.
2. The capital of Mexico is Tenochtitlan.
3. Tenochtitlan was a very small town when the Spaniards arrived.
4. **Los mestizos** are groups of Mexican musicians who sing traditional songs.
5. The Aztecs built Mexico City on a site where they saw two snakes.

¿Adónde vas hoy?

Objetivos

- To learn the days of the week
- To talk about going places
- To talk about where you go on different days of the week

Cuahutemoc Station of the
Mexico City subway system

A group of friends buys movie tickets in Los Angeles.

1 ENERO

L	M	M	J	V	S	D
○7	(15	●21	)29	1	2	3
4	5	6	7	8	9	10
11	12	13	14	15	16	17
18	19	20	21	22	23	24
25	26	27	28	29	30	31

1-AÑO NUEVO • 6-REYES

A calendar from Argentina

¿Sabías que...?

In Spanish-speaking countries:

- School days tend to be longer since students usually have more subjects—sometimes up to ten a day!

- Calendars usually start on Mondays, rather than on Sundays.

- When you go to a park, you can almost always find kids playing **fútbol**—soccer.

- People like to celebrate birthdays in parks, and to go to parks with their family on weekends.

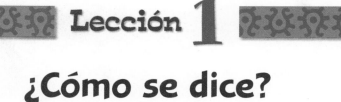

¿Cómo se dice?

What are the days of the week?

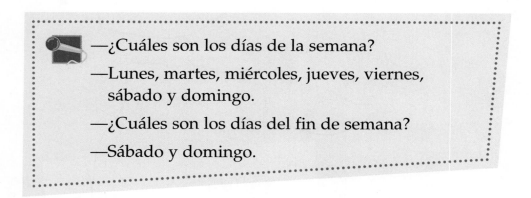

—¿Cuáles son los días de la semana?

—Lunes, martes, miércoles, jueves, viernes, sábado y domingo.

—¿Cuáles son los días del fin de semana?

—Sábado y domingo.

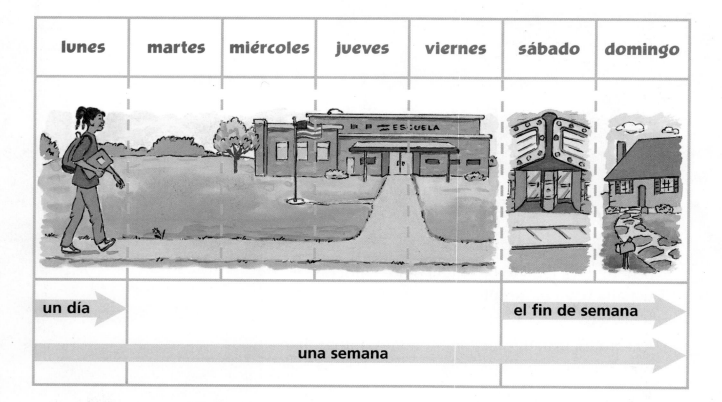

lunes	martes	miércoles	jueves	viernes	sábado	domingo

un día →

el fin de semana →

una semana →

El lunes means "this Monday." **Los lunes** means "on Mondays" or "every Monday."

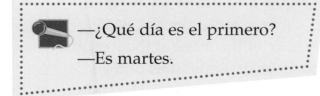

—¿Qué día es hoy? ¿Lunes?

—Sí, y mañana es martes, ¡claro!

el calendario

lunes	martes	miércoles	jueves	viernes	sábado	domingo
	1 X el primero	2 X	3 X	4 X	5 X	6 X
7 hoy	8 mañana	9	10	11	12	13
14	15	16	17	18	19	20
21	22	23	24	25	26	27
28	29	30 el treinta	31 el treinta y uno			

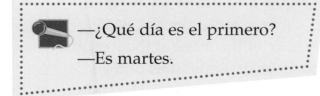

—¿Qué día es el primero?

—Es martes.

¿Sabías que...?

In Spanish, the first letter of the days of the week is not capitalized.

¡Úsalo!

A Get together with a partner. Write the seven days of the week on cards. Shuffle the cards and hand them to your partner. Your partner puts them in order, starting with today. Use these questions to get started. Then switch roles and start again.

¿Qué día es hoy? ¿Qué día es mañana?

¿Cuáles son los días de la semana? ¿Cuáles son los días del fin de semana?

B Draw a calendar for next month with the days of the week across the top. You need to know what days fall on certain dates, but you don't have a calendar. Ask a partner who is looking at a ready-made calendar. Fill in your calendar according to your partner's answers. After finishing, double-check with your partner.

Partner A: Ask what day of the week a certain date is.

Partner B: Look at the calendar and answer.

> **MODELO** —¿Qué día es el tres?
>
> —Es domingo.

CONEXIÓN CON LA SALUD

Health and Fitness Diary Keep a health and fitness diary for a week. Use seven sheets of paper or index cards to make the pages of your diary. Start by writing in Spanish the day of the week at the top of each page. Then, every day for a week, paste or draw pictures of the physical activity that you did each day. Try to plan ahead to make sure that you get in some physical activity every day. You can include sports, walking, dancing, doing chores around the house, and any other activity that keeps you moving!

C At the zoo, each animal is scheduled for a medical checkup once a month. The zoo worker on duty takes the animal to the vet. Get together with a partner. Ask him or her what day of the week is each date, according to the calendar. Your partner tells you the day of the week. You say the name of the zoo worker on duty that day who will take the animal to the vet.

Fecha	Nombre
Día 2: el pez	_____
Día 7: el flamenco	_____
Día 10: el oso	_____
Día 18: el tigre	_____
Día 20: el loro	

The zoo workers work on the following days:

Javier	**lunes, miércoles y viernes**
Lina	**martes y jueves**
Ricardo	**sábado y domingo**

MODELO —¿Qué día es el dos?

—Es jueves.

lunes	martes	miércoles	jueves	viernes	sábado	domingo
		1	2	3	4	5
6	7	8	9	10	11	12
13	14	15	16	17	18	19
20	21	22	23	24	25	26
27	28	28	30			

For this game, you'll need a chalkboard or large "scoreboard," and a tennis ball or other lightweight ball.

Choose a scorekeeper. Then form two teams. A player from Team A starts by saying a day of the week, and throws the ball to any player from Team B. That player must name the day that follows:

> **Team A Player:** —Sábado.

> **Team B Player:** —Domingo.

If the player answers correctly, Team B scores a point. That same player says a new day of the week, and throws the ball to any player from Team A. (You may wish to change the rules after a while, and name the day that comes before.)

The team that scores the most points wins.

En resumen

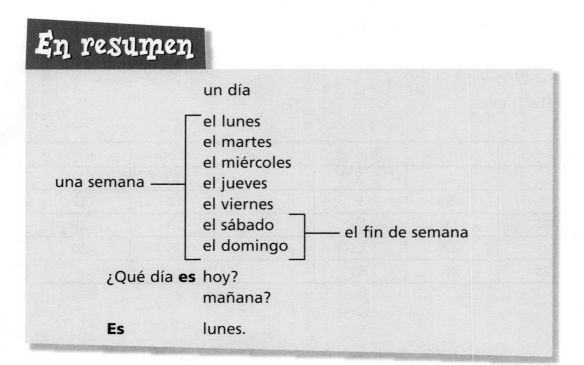

un día

una semana —
- el lunes
- el martes
- el miércoles
- el jueves
- el viernes
- el sábado ⎤
- el domingo ⎦ — el fin de semana

¿Qué día **es** hoy?
mañana?

Es lunes.

¿Cómo se dice?

Where are you going?

> —¿Adónde vas el lunes?
> —Voy a la escuela.

la escuela

la casa

la tienda

el cine

el parque

el calendario

lunes	martes	miércoles	jueves	viernes	sábado	domingo
	1 X	2 X	3 X	4 X	5 X	6 X
7 hoy	8	9	**esta semana**		2	13
14	15	**la próxima semana**				20
21	22	23	24	25	26	27
28	29	30				

—¿Cuándo vas al cine?

—Voy el domingo. *or* Voy esta semana. *or* Voy este fin de semana.

¿Sabías que...?

It is common for stores to close on Sundays in some Spanish-speaking countries. In many smaller towns and rural areas, everything may close down on Sundays. During weekdays, businesses may close for two to three hours in the afternoon for a long lunch and some rest. Store hours in many cities, however, are starting to resemble those in the United States.

¡Úsalo!

A You're going to different places. In each place you go, you will see one of the following things. Work with a partner and ask each other **¿Adónde vas?** Answer using the words and pictures.

MODELO Voy al _____.

Voy al parque.

1. Voy a la _____.

2. Voy al _____.

3. Voy a la _____.

4. Voy a la _____.

CONEXIÓN CON LOS ESTUDIOS SOCIALES

Making Maps and Keys Draw a map of your town or an imaginary town. Work with a partner to create a map key. Make up different symbols to represent buildings and places, including a park, a school, a movie theater, stores, and houses.

You will need to decide on a different color for each symbol. In order to make these decisions, ask your partner questions such as **¿De qué color es la escuela?** Your partner says a color and you color in the symbol. Then switch roles with your partner.

el zoo =

Compara

En inglés	En español
symbol	el símbolo

¿Sabías que...?

Most cities and towns in the Spanish-speaking world have a central **plaza** or square, surrounded by some of the most important buildings in town. Look at Plaza Murillo in La Paz, Bolivia. What does the center of your town look like? Does it look like Plaza Murillo? What parts are similar? What parts are different?

Entre amigos

See if you and your friends have similar schedules. Make a chart like this one:

¿Cuándo vas...	¿Hoy?	¿Mañana?	¿El fin de semana?	¿Esta semana?	¿La próxima semana?
al cine?	✔				
a la tienda?					
al parque?					
a la escuela?					
a la casa de un(a) amigo(a)?					

Think of when you would like to go to each of these places. Put a check mark in each box that applies to you. Then get together with four or five classmates. Ask them the questions to see if they planned similar schedules.

¿Cuándo vas al cine?
¿Hoy?
¿Mañana?
¿Esta semana?
¿El fin de semana?
¿La próxima semana?

En resumen

¿Adónde **vas?**
   Voy a la casa.
         a la escuela.
         a la tienda.
         al cine.
         al parque.

¿Cuándo **vas?**
   Voy esta semana.
         la próxima semana.

¿Cómo se dice?

Talking about going places

Look at the pictures. What words tell where the people are going?

Voy **a la** escuela.

Voy **al** parque.

Voy **al** cine.

Voy **al** salón de clase.

Voy **a la** tienda.

Voy **a la** casa de José.

Did you notice that some sentences have **al** and some sentences have **a la?**

In Spanish, when you talk about going to places, use **al** for words with **el:**

> **el parque** ➡ **Voy al parque.**

Use **a la** for words with **la:**

> **la tienda** ➡ **Voy a la tienda.**

¡Úsalo!

Get together with a partner. Together you'll make drawings of **el cine, el parque, la tienda, la casa,** and **la escuela** on different sheets of paper, and write the names of these five places on different sheets of paper. Put all the sheets of paper facedown in two piles. You pick a word and your partner picks a drawing. Look at the place name and ask your partner if he or she is going there. Your partner looks at the drawing and answers according to the place he or she has picked. Then switch roles.

> **MODELO** —¿Vas al parque?
>
> —Sí. *or* No, voy a la escuela.

¿Sabías que...?

Puerto Rico, which is a commonwealth of the United States, is home to the only tropical rain forest ecosystem in the U.S. national forest system. This tropical rain forest is called **El Yunque.** Originally set aside while Puerto Rico was still part of Spain, it is one of the oldest protected areas in the Western Hemisphere.

CONEXIÓN CON EL ARTE

Dubbing and Subtitles American movies are popular throughout the Spanish-speaking world. In some countries, American movies are *dubbed.* This means that Spanish-speaking actors record their voices over those of English-speaking characters. In other places, the movies have *subtitles,* which are words at the bottom of the screen that translate into Spanish the words that the characters speak in English. Have you ever seen a movie in a different language with English subtitles? What was the original language of the movie?

¿Sabías que...?

Many people in Latin America like to paint their houses in very bright and different colors, inside and out! What color would you paint your room if you could pick any one?

Entre amigos

Interview six classmates to find out where they go on weekends—to the movies, to the park, to the store, or just to their house. Write their names on a chart like the one below and place a check mark under their answer.

—¿Adónde vas los fines de semana?
—Voy al cine.

Nombre	el cine	el parque	la tienda	la casa
Linda	✔			

Depending on the answers, you can ask some follow-up questions, and write those answers down as well.

¿Cuál es tu tienda favorita?
¿Cómo se llama tu cine favorito? ¿Es grande o pequeño?
¿De qué color es tu casa? ¿Cómo es tu casa? ¿Es grande o pequeña?

Add up all the check marks and compare your results with those of a partner. What's the most popular place to go on weekends?

En resumen

¿**Vas** al parque?
 No **voy** al parque. **Voy** a la escuela.

Voy a + **el** parque ➔ Voy **al** parque.
Voy a + **la** casa ➔ Voy **a la** casa.

Lección 4

¿Cómo se dice?

Who's going?

In each set of sentences, which words are different?

Voy a la escuela.

Vas a la escuela.

Va a la escuela.

Voy al cine.

¿Vas al cine?

Va al cine.

In each picture, the *person* who is going changes. Use **voy** to talk about yourself, **vas** to talk to your brothers, sisters, and other kids, and **va** to talk about another person. **Voy, vas,** and **va** are all forms of the verb **ir,** which means "to go."

¡Úsalo!

Your partner wants to know where your friends are going on certain days. You just happen to have a calendar of their activities.

	Elena	**Jaime**	**María**	**Jorge**
lunes	la casa	la escuela	la escuela	la escuela
martes	la escuela	la escuela	la escuela	la escuela
miércoles	la escuela	el parque	la escuela	la tienda
jueves	el parque	la escuela	la escuela	la escuela
viernes	la tienda	el parque	la tienda	el cine
sábado	la casa	la escuela	el cine	el parque
domingo	el cine	el cine	el parque	la casa

Partner A: Ask the question.

Partner B: Answer according to the schedule.

> **MODELO** —¿Va Elena a la escuela el lunes?
>
> —No, no va a la escuela. Va a la casa.

1. ¿Va Jaime al cine el sábado?

2. ¿Va María a la casa el martes?

3. ¿Va Jorge a la tienda el viernes?

4. ¿Va Elena al parque el viernes?

5. ¿Va Jorge al cine el lunes?

6. ¿Va Jaime a la tienda el domingo?

7. ¿Va María al parque el miércoles?

8. ¿Va Elena al cine el sábado?

Entre amigos

Everyone is going to the movies on Friday!

Prepare four cards with a partner. On the first one, write your own name. On the second one, write your partner's name. On the third one, write **Rosa.** On the fourth one, write **Carlos.**

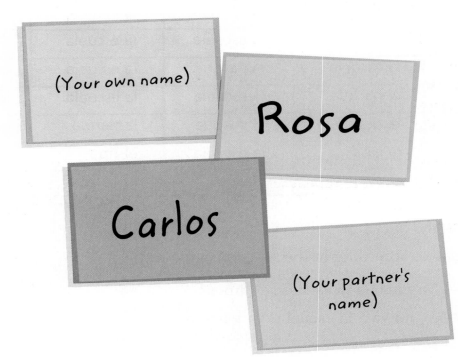

Shuffle the cards and pick one. If you get your own name, tell your partner that *you're* going to the movies on Friday. If you get your partner's name, tell your partner that *he* or *she* is going to the movies on Friday. If you get **Rosa** or **Carlos,** tell your partner that *Rosa* or *Carlos* is going to the movies on Friday.

Take turns picking cards. When you have gone through all of the cards, pick a different day of the week and a different destination and start over!

CONEXIÓN CON LOS ESTUDIOS SOCIALES

Are you good at writing events on a calendar? Form a circle with four other classmates. Each person will use a blank calendar for the next two weeks to take notes.

One person starts by asking the next player where he or she is going and when. The second player answers.

—**¿Adónde vas?**
—**Voy al cine.**
—**¿Cuándo vas al cine?**
—**Voy (hoy, esta semana, la próxima semana, el lunes, el fin de semana, el 24, etc.).**

As people answer, write down their names and activities on your calendar. Ask them to repeat where they're going if you need to. Go around the circle until everyone has had a chance to ask and answer both questions.

Now everyone in the group should take out a sheet of paper and write down where and when the other people are going, based on the notes each of you took on your calendar.

Jorge va a la tienda la próxima semana. Carmen va...

Compare sentences to see who took the best notes!

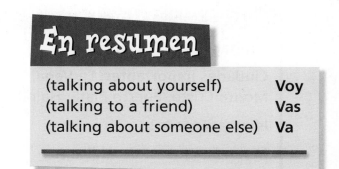

En resumen

(talking about yourself)	**Voy**
(talking to a friend)	**Vas**
(talking about someone else)	**Va**

¿Dónde se habla español?

LA REPÚBLICA DOMINICANA

Santo Domingo

La República Dominicana

Dominican culture is the product of the mixture of three cultures: Spanish, African, and Taíno. Taíno is the culture of the native inhabitants of the island. In 1492, Christopher Columbus arrived on the island, which he named Hispaniola. Today, this island is divided into two countries: two thirds of the island is the Dominican Republic, and one third is Haiti. The Dominican Republic was the first European colony in the Americas. As such, it claims the first forts, churches, hospital, and university in the Americas. Some typical products of the Dominican Republic are **muñecas de limé,** which are special dolls with anonymous faces and long dresses, and amber, a beautiful yellowish golden stone. The popular music, **merengue,** combines instruments of indigenous groups **(el güiro),** Africans **(la tambora),** and Europeans **(el acordeón** and **el cuatro).** You can see a güiro on the next page. **Carnaval** is the biggest festival celebrated in the Dominican Republic; it is usually celebrated in late February.

Beautiful waterfalls, beaches, and parks await visitors, who can also try typical dishes, such as sweet potato fritters, sweet potato **flan** and **sancocho,** a type of stew. One of the best-known Dominicans in the United States is baseball player Sammy Sosa.

◎ ◎ ◎ ◎ Datos ◎ ◎ ◎ ◎

Capital: Santo Domingo

Ciudades importantes: La Vega, Monte Cristo, Puerto Plata, Haina

Idioma: Español

Moneda: El peso dominicano

Población: 8.7 millones

¡Léelo en español!

Las ballenas jorobadas En los meses de enero, febrero y marzo, entre 300 y 3,000 ballenas jorobadas[1] vienen a Samaná. Los machos[2] saltan del agua, se levantan y gritan. Las ballenas han venido[3] por más de 500 años. Han venido antes de Cristóbal Colón. A las ballenas les gusta Samaná porque el agua es caliente y tranquila. Algunas ballenas nadan por 8,000 millas para viajar a Samaná. Los turistas pueden ir en barco a ver las ballenas, pero hay reglas[4] muy estrictas para proteger a las ballenas. Por ejemplo, un barco no puede estar con las ballenas por más de treinta minutos.

[1] humpback whales   [2] males   [3] have come
[4] rules

Reading Strategy

Using Context Clues Titles are important. Read titles carefully and be sure you know what they mean before you begin reading. Titles are your most important clue to the theme of the reading. How can reading the title of this selection and examining the accompanying photograph help you understand it better?

Recognizing Cognates What do you think these words mean: **tranquila, estrictas?** Use these cognates to help you understand what is being said about the humpback whales.

¡Comprendo!

Answer in English.

1. What are the cultures that have combined to create modern-day Dominican culture? What are some examples of how these cultures have become intermingled?

2. Why do humpback whales come to Samaná? What do they do there?

3. What is done to protect the whales in Samaná?

En la escuela

Objetivos

- To talk about your classes
- To talk about other places in your school
- To talk about what you're going to do
- To talk about school activities

A music class in Chile

Children learn to use computers in a class in Mexico City.

Children work on a class mural.

¿Sabías que...?

- In many Spanish-speaking countries, there are special schools where students go just to study music.

- Many schools are decorated with beautiful murals, some of them painted by students.

- In some places, **la escuela** is called **el colegio.** The names for *middle school* and *high school* also vary by country.

¿Cómo se dice?

Where are you going?

CONEXIÓN CON EL ARTE

Diego Rivera Diego Rivera was an artist from Mexico who painted murals about Mexican life. A mural is a painting made on a wall. The artists who paint them are called *muralists.* Rivera painted many large murals on public buildings. Look at his mural called **"La Zafra."** Work with your class to paint a mural of your own on a large sheet of paper in your classroom.

¡Úsalo!

A Get together with a partner. Imagine that these are your class schedules **(horarios)** for the week. Choose one schedule each. Ask each other questions about your schedules.

> **MODELO** —¿Adónde vas el lunes?
>
> —Voy a la clase de música y a la clase de arte.

Horario A

Horario B

B Write some notes like these about where you'll be on three days this week.

lunes
la escuela
la clase de música
la biblioteca

miércoles
la escuela
el gimnasio
la clase de arte
la tienda

viernes
la escuela
el gimnasio
la clase de computadoras
el cine

Get together with a partner and ask each other questions like these: **¿Adónde vas el lunes? ¿Cuándo vas a la clase de arte? ¿Vas al gimnasio el viernes? ¿Vas a la tienda el lunes? ¿Vas a la clase de música esta semana?**
Based on your partner's answers, make a schedule for his or her week. Have your partner check the schedule to see if it is correct.

CONEXIÓN CON LAS MATEMÁTICAS

Fractions Interview everyone in your class to find out their favorite place in school. Keep track of their answers on a chart like this one. Then find the fraction of the class that prefers each place. What is the most popular place in school?

	Total de alumnos = 35	Fracción
biblioteca	✔ ✔ ✔ = 3	3/35
clase de arte		
clase de música		
clase de computadoras		
gimnasio		

En resumen

¿Adónde **vas?**
  Voy a la biblioteca.
       a la clase de arte.
       a la clase de computadoras.
       a la clase de música.
       al gimnasio.

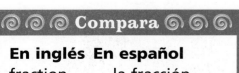

ⓒ ⓒ ⓒ **Compara** ⓒ ⓒ ⓒ

En inglés	En español
fraction	la fracción
total	el total

¿Cómo se dice?

What are you going to do?

¿Qué vas a hacer?

Voy a pintar.

pintar

estudiar

cantar

usar la computadora

practicar deportes

hablar

escuchar

participar

trabajar

¿Sabías que...?

The names of many sports are very similar in English and Spanish. Some don't even change at all! Can you tell what sports these are? **(Hint:** Try saying them out loud!)

el tenis
el básquetbol
el voleibol
el softball

el béisbol
el fútbol americano
el boxeo

¡Úsalo!

A Draw a map of your school. Label the places you know in Spanish, including your classroom. Then write these activities on separate cards.

cantar
pintar
usar la computadora
practicar deportes
estudiar

Mix up the cards, put them facedown, and pick one. Your partner asks you what you're going to do. Answer according to the card. Your partner draws a line on the map from your classroom to the place you need to go to do that activity. Is your partner right?

MODELO —¿Qué vas a hacer?

—Voy a pintar.

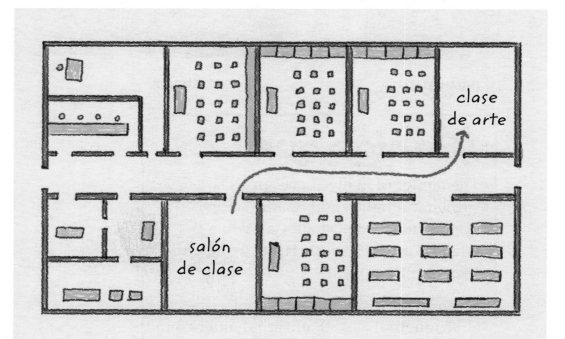

After picking all the cards and "going" to all the places, switch roles with your partner and start again.

B Write the names of these places on separate cards. Mix the cards and put them facedown. Then get together with two or three classmates and pick a card. Pretend to do an activity in that place. Your classmates have to guess what you're doing. Take turns acting out and guessing activities.

la clase de computadoras

el salón de clase

la clase de música

el gimnasio

la clase de arte

la biblioteca

CONEXIÓN CON LA MÚSICA

Mariachi Groups Mariachi groups play and sing at weddings, birthday parties, and other events in Mexican and Mexican American communities. They have been entertaining audiences for over 200 years. These groups used to be made up mostly of string players, like guitarists and violinists, but today they include trumpet players and others. What musical traditions are there in your town or state?

Entre amigos

How well do your friends know you?

Make a list of the five school activities you just learned. List the activity you most enjoy first, and give it 5 points. Then list your next favorite, and give it 4 points, and so on. Here's an example:

cantar—5
pintar—4
usar la computadora—3
practicar deportes—2
estudiar—1

Without showing your list, ask a partner **¿Qué voy a hacer?**

Your partner will answer **Vas a...** three times, naming the three activities that he or she thinks you like most. After your partner answers, add up the points you gave to the activities that he or she named. Then switch roles with your partner and you answer the question, trying to guess your partner's favorite activities. When you finish, compare point totals. Which of you knows the other better?

En resumen

¿Qué **vas** a hacer?
    Voy a cantar.
          escuchar.
          estudiar.
          hablar.
          participar.
          pintar.
          practicar deportes.
          trabajar.
          usar la computadora.

¿Cómo se dice?

What are people going to do?

Here's how to say different people are going to do something:

Voy a pintar.   **¿Vas a** pintar?   **Va a** pintar.

Voy a estudiar.   **¿Vas a** estudiar?   **Va a** estudiar.

To say that someone is going to do something, you use **voy a, vas a,** or **va a** plus another verb that tells what the person is going to do.

¡Úsalo!

A With a partner, draw a map of your school on butcher paper. Write the name of each room on the map. Cut out six "people" from construction paper and label them with names. Then place the "people" in different rooms, and ask your partner what they will do. Your partner answers by looking at the "people" on the school map. Then it's your partner's turn to move the "people" around and ask you what they will do.

> **MODELO** —¿Qué va a hacer José?
>
> —Va a estudiar en la biblioteca.

B Fill out a chart like this one. Choose four things to do tomorrow, and four to do next week.

	mañana	**la próxima semana**
ir al gimnasio		
trabajar		
usar la computadora		
ir al cine		
pintar		
cantar		
practicar deportes		
estudiar		

Then get together with a partner. Your partner asks you whether you will do each thing tomorrow. Answer according to what you wrote on your chart.

> **MODELO** —¿Vas a ir al gimnasio mañana?
>
> —No, no voy a ir al gimnasio mañana. Voy a ir la próxima semana.

Play "Telephone" in the classroom! Stand in line with three or four classmates.

Your teacher will ask the first student what he or she is doing tomorrow: **¿Qué vas a hacer mañana, Alicia?** and will hand the first student a card with a picture of an activity or a place. Based on this picture, the first student whispers his or her answer in the second student's ear: **Voy a (estudiar en la biblioteca).** Then the second student whispers in the third student's ear what the first student is doing tomorrow: **Alicia va a estudiar en la biblioteca.** The last student says out loud what he or she heard. The first student must make any corrections.

Take turns being first in line. Each time the teacher asks a question, a new day or week will be used and activities and places will vary. See how fast the message gets through!

CONEXIÓN CON LAS MATEMÁTICAS

Ordering Numbers It's the beginning of the school year, and students have signed up to do different activities. Look at the following activities and write them in order, from the one with the most students to the one with the least.

Cincuenta y ocho alumnos van a ir a la clase de música.
Cuarenta alumnos van a usar las computadoras.
Treinta y cinco alumnos van a practicar deportes.
Sesenta y cuatro alumnos van a estudiar en la biblioteca.
Dieciséis alumnos van a cantar.
Veintidós alumnos van a ir a la clase de arte.
Cincuenta y tres alumnos van a pintar.

Compare your results with a partner.

¿Sabías que...?

In many Spanish-speaking countries, students don't have the chance to take part in extracurricular activities at school. Instead, they may go to a cultural center or workshop to learn photography, dance, or music.

En resumen

Voy a pintar.
Vas a pintar.
Va a pintar.

¿Cómo se dice?

What do you do in your classes?

Here's how you can use words like **pintar, estudiar, cantar,** and **hablar** to tell what people do.

Pint**o** muy bien.

Pint**as** muy bien.

Pint**a** muy bien.

Estudi**o** mucho.

Estudi**as** mucho.

Luis estudi**a** mucho.

Canto en la clase.   Cantas en la clase.   Iris canta en la clase.

Hablo mucho.   Hablas mucho.   Habla mucho.

Action words, or verbs, have different endings to show who is doing the action. With verbs that end in **-ar,** use the **-o** ending to talk about yourself, the **-as** ending to talk to a friend, and the **-a** ending to talk about another person.

You can also talk about *how* a person does something. If the person does something *very well*, you can say:

Pinta **muy bien.**

If the person does something *a lot*, you can say:

Estudia **mucho.**

¡Úsalo!

A You're showing your little brother some photos of friends at school. As you show him each picture, say the person's name and what that person does.

MODELO **Marta practica deportes.**

Marta

1. **Ramón**
2. **Jorge**
3. **Victoria**
4. **Bárbara**

B Your little brother asks so many questions! He wants to know about your activities in and around school. Work with a partner and answer his questions.

Partner A: Ask the question.

Partner B: Answer each question.

MODELO —¿Estudias mucho en la clase de arte?

—Sí, estudio mucho en la clase de arte.

1. ¿Estudias mucho los fines de semana?
2. ¿Practicas deportes los lunes?
3. ¿Estudias en la biblioteca?
4. ¿Hablas mucho en el salón de clase?
5. ¿Participas mucho en la clase de arte?
6. ¿Usas la computadora en la clase de música?

C Write the activities below on separate cards. Then get together with a partner. Each of you mixes your cards and puts them facedown in a pile. Pick a card from your pile and ask the question. Your partner picks a card from his or her pile and answers according to what is on it. Then switch roles.

Partner A: Ask the question according to your card.

Partner B: Pick a card and answer accordingly.

> **MODELO** —¿Cantas en la clase de música?
>
> —Sí, canto en la clase de música.
>   *or* No, estudio en la biblioteca.

1. cantar en la clase de música
2. pintar en la clase de arte
3. estudiar en la biblioteca
4. trabajar en la casa
5. usar la computadora en la clase de computadoras

D Look at these school activities. For each one, think of one classmate who does the activity a lot, and another classmate who doesn't. Write sentences like those shown below.

estudiar	pintar	cantar	usar la computadora
hablar	escuchar	participar	trabajar

> **MODELO** Carlos usa mucho la computadora.
>
> Analía no usa mucho la computadora.

Are you right about your classmates? To find out, ask them.

> **MODELO** —Carlos, ¿usas mucho la computadora?
>
> —Sí, uso mucho la computadora.
>   *or* No, no uso mucho la computadora.

Entre amigos

Write an article for a class newspaper. Interview a classmate. Ask at least three questions about his or her activities, and then write a paragraph. Here's an example:

¿Cuáles son tus clases favoritas?
¿Cuándo vas a tus clases favoritas?
¿Adónde vas los fines de semana?
¿Participas mucho en las clases?

> *Las clases favoritas de Raúl son la música y el arte. Va a la clase de música los lunes, los martes, los jueves y los viernes. Va a la clase de arte los miércoles. No va a la escuela los fines de semana. Los fines de semana va al cine y a las tiendas.*

Exchange papers with another classmate. Read your classmate's paragraph and give ideas for any changes. Make the changes before you submit your paragraph to the newspaper editor (your teacher).

En resumen

	(yourself)	(to a friend)	(about someone else)
cantar	canto	cantas	canta
escuchar	escucho	escuchas	escucha
estudiar	estudio	estudias	estudia
hablar	hablo	hablas	habla
participar	participo	participas	participa
pintar	pinto	pintas	pinta
practicar	practico	practicas	practica
trabajar	trabajo	trabajas	trabaja
usar	uso	usas	usa
muy bien			
mucho			

¿Dónde se habla español?

Costa Rica

When you think of nature and conservation, think of Costa Rica. This small Central American country has many nature preserves where you can hike and see protected animals and plants. About 27 percent of the country is set aside to protect nature in one form or another. Costa Rica has the largest number of the magnificent **quetzal** bird of any country, as well as many other species of birds, mammals, reptiles, and insects. You can also find beautiful beaches, volcanoes, hot springs, and mountains to climb. White-water rafting is popular, too. This is the perfect place for nature lovers.

@ @ @ @ @ @ **Datos** @ @ @ @ @ @

Capital: San José

Ciudades importantes: Cartago, Puerto Limón, Puntarenas, Alajuela

Idiomas: Español y lenguas indígenas

Moneda: El colón

Población: 3.9 millones

¡Léelo en español!

El volcán Arenal y la Reserva Monteverde El volcán Arenal está situado[1] en el centro de Costa Rica cerca del pueblo La Fortuna. Es un volcán activo y puedes ver las erupciones. Por la noche, el cielo *se pone*[2] anaranjado con sus fuegos. La lava sale del volcán y el volcán echa piedras del centro al aire afuera. No puedes subir el volcán, pero hay lugares[3] donde puedes caminar para verlo mejor.

La Reserva Biológica Monteverde es otro lugar impresionante[4] en Costa Rica. Es una de las muchas reservas, que son parques especiales donde las plantas y los animales están protegidos[5]. Hay muchas sendas[6] donde puedes caminar. Allí ves muchos pájaros y con suerte puedes ver el magnífico quetzal. También puedes ver mariposas, serpientes, picaflores[7] y jardines de orquídeas[8]. Es un paraíso natural.

Reading Strategy

Using Visuals Look carefully at the pictures. What do you see in them? What do you know about volcanoes? What do you know about nature preserves? Use this information to help you understand the reading.

Recognizing Cognates What do you think these words mean: **volcán, erupciones, lava, paraíso?** Use these cognates to help you understand what is being said about Costa Rica.

¡Comprendo!

Answer in English.

1. What are three things you learned about the country of Costa Rica?

2. Describe Monteverde. Would you like to hike there? What would you expect to see?

3. Describe the live volcano Arenal. Would you like to see it? Why?

4. List ten things you might be able to see in Costa Rica.

¿Qué estación te gusta?

Objetivos

- To learn about the seasons
- To talk about different kinds of weather
- To talk about what you like and don't like
- To use descriptive words to name the things you like

Manuel Antonio National Park in Costa Rica

A skier enjoys Mount Aconcagua in the Andes Mountains of Argentina.

Lime Cay Beach, Belice

¿Sabías que...?

- January is a popular month to go to the beach in Argentina. It's usually around 80° Fahrenheit.

- The climate in Perú varies greatly, from steaming, hot jungles to snowy mountaintops that are always frozen.

- Several Spanish-speaking countries in Central and South America, as well as in the Caribbean, are in the tropics. It feels like summer all year long!

- In some tropical countries, it gets colder in areas that are high up in the mountains.

¿Cómo se dice?

 **What season do you like?**

¿Qué estación te gusta?

Me gusta el verano.

el verano

el otoño

el invierno

la primavera

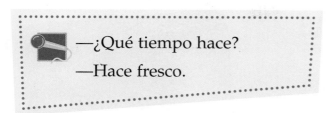

—¿Qué tiempo hace?

—Hace fresco.

Hace fresco.

Hace frío.

Hace sol.

Hace calor.

Nieva.

Llueve.

CONEXIÓN CON LAS CIENCIAS

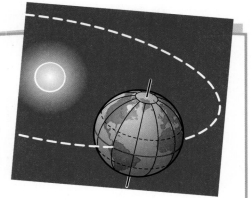

The Equator As you know, the equator **(el ecuador)** divides the world into the Northern Hemisphere and the Southern Hemisphere. Places close to the equator have similar seasons. The differences become greater as you go farther away from the equator. For example, it's summer in Chile and Argentina in December when it's winter in the United States. That's because the southern half of the Earth tilts toward the sun in the winter, while the northern half tilts away from the sun. And when you're enjoying warm summer days in the United States, what season is it in Chile and Argentina?

¿Sabías que...?

The country of **Ecuador** is named after its location. The equator runs through the country at a point very close to the capital city of Quito. There is a monument marking this location. It's called **La Mitad del Mundo** (*The Middle of the*

World). Here, you can stand with one foot in the Northern Hemisphere and one foot in the Southern Hemisphere.

ecuador

ECUADOR

América del Sur

¡Úsalo!

A Each of these pictures was taken during a different season. Get together with a partner and take turns asking **¿Qué estación es?**

Partner A: Ask what season it is.

Partner B: Answer according to the picture.

1.

2.

3.

4.

B What is the weather like where you live? Get together with a partner and use all the weather expressions that apply for each season.

(No) Hace calor.	(No) Hace sol.	(No) Hace fresco.
(No) Hace frío.	(No) Llueve.	(No) Nieva.

1. En primavera...   **2.** En verano...   **3.** En invierno...   **4.** En otoño...

CONEXIÓN CON LOS ESTUDIOS SOCIALES

Weather Map Look at the weather map. Make a map key that shows the Spanish meaning of each symbol. Then take turns asking a partner questions about the weather in each city.

MODELO —¿Qué tiempo hace en Buenos Aires?

—Hace sol.

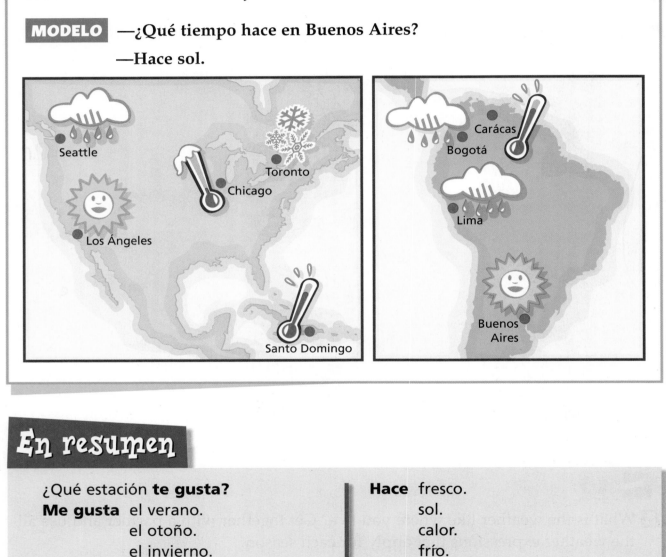

En resumen

¿Qué estación **te gusta?**
Me gusta el verano.
el otoño.
el invierno.
la primavera.

¿Qué tiempo **hace** en otoño?
invierno?
primavera?
verano?

Hace fresco.
sol.
calor.
frío.
Llueve.
Nieva.

¿Cómo se dice?

What's the weather like now?

—¿Qué tiempo hace ahora?

—Está nevando.

Hace buen tiempo.

Hace mal tiempo. / Está lloviendo.

Está nublado.

Hace viento.

CONEXIÓN CON LAS CIENCIAS

El Niño A very interesting weather event occurs off the western coast of South America every four to twelve years. It is called **El Niño.** As a result of **El Niño,** the surface of the ocean warms. It causes plankton and fish to die and affects weather over much of the Pacific Ocean. Sometimes it even causes terrible hurricanes. Why do you think it's called **El Niño?**

¿Sabías que...?

The word *hurricane* comes from the language of the **taíno** natives of the Caribbean. The ancient **taíno** tribe believed in a god of evil named **Juracán.** They believed that when this god became angry, he would send powerful storms their way. The Spanish word for hurricane is **huracán.**

⊚ ⊚ ⊚ ⊚ ⊚ Compara ⊚ ⊚ ⊚ ⊚ ⊚

En inglés	En español
hurricane	el huracán
Caribbean	el Caribe
Pacific Ocean	el océano Pacífico

¡Úsalo!

Fill out a questionnaire about the weather where you live. Write your answers on a separate sheet of paper. Compare your answers with a partner.

1. ¿Hace buen tiempo en la primavera?
2. ¿Hace viento en el verano?
3. ¿Hace calor en el verano?
4. ¿Nieva en el invierno?
5. ¿Hace fresco en el otoño?
6. ¿Llueve en la primavera?
7. ¿Hace mal tiempo en el otoño?
8. ¿Qué tiempo hace ahora?

Entre amigos

Make a calendar like this one. For one week, keep track of the weather where you live. Then get together with a partner and compare your calendars. Did you observe the same kinds of weather?

lunes	martes	miércoles	jueves	viernes	sábado	domingo

CONEXIÓN CON LAS CIENCIAS

Temperature Work with three classmates. Pick a city from these newspaper clippings. Talk about the weather and Celsius temperature there during the month of January. (Use **grados** to say *degrees.*) Don't say the name of the city. Your classmates ask questions and guess the name of the city.

MODELO —Hace sol.

—¿Hace calor?

—Sí, hace treinta grados Celsius.

—¿Es Buenos Aires?

Miami
25°C/77°F

Buenos Aires
30°C/86°F

Chicago
1°C/34°F

Madrid
10°C/50°F

Santo Domingo
36°C/97°F

Dallas
15°C/59°F

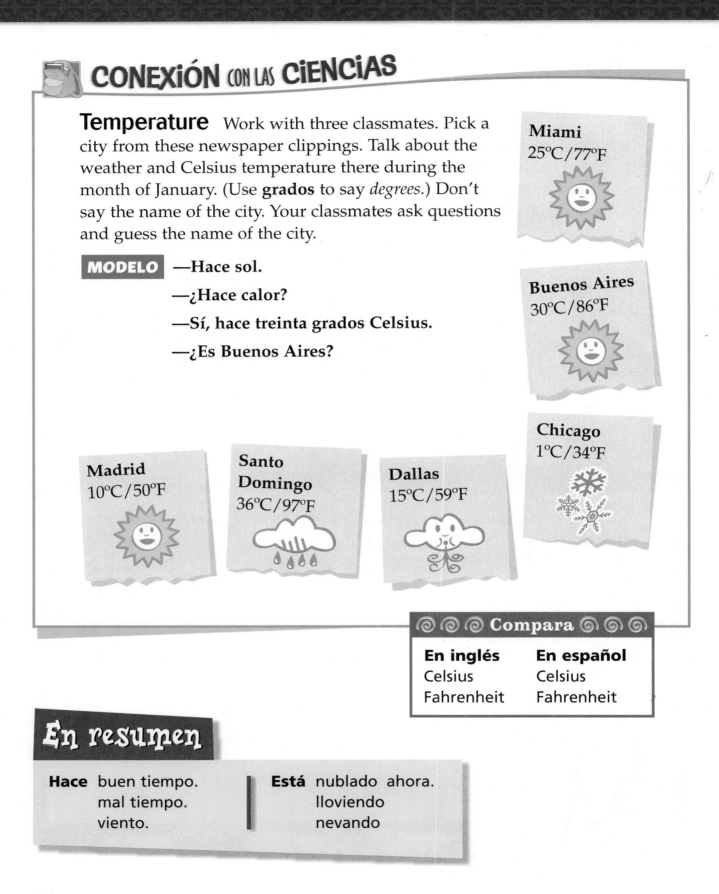

◎ ◎ ◎ ⊙ Compara ◎ ◎ ◎ ◎

En inglés	En español
Celsius	Celsius
Fahrenheit	Fahrenheit

En resumen

Hace	buen tiempo.	**Está**	nublado ahora.
	mal tiempo.		lloviendo
	viento.		nevando

¿Cómo se dice?

Talking about likes and dislikes

How do you say you like something? Look at these sentences to find out.

Me gusta pintar.

¿Te gusta pintar?

A Juan le gusta pintar.

Me gusta el verano.

¿Te gusta el verano?

A Delia le gusta
el verano.

Did you notice that the same word (**gusta**) is used in all the sentences?
In each sentence, how do you know who likes something?

The words **me, te,** and **le** give you that information. You use **me gusta** to talk about yourself, **te gusta** to talk to a friend, and **le gusta** to talk about someone else.

Talking about dislikes works the same way:

No me gusta cantar.

¿No te gusta pintar?

A Víctor no le gusta el invierno.

Look back at the different sentences in this section. What's different about the sentences with the names Juan, Delia, and Víctor?

If you mention someone's name when talking about that person's likes and dislikes, you need to use the word **a** before the person you are talking about. If it's clear who you're talking about, you do not have to mention the person's name again.

A Susana no le gusta el invierno.
No le gusta el frío.

A la maestra le gusta el verano.
Le gusta nadar.

¡Úsalo!

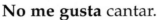

A Get together with three or four classmates and make charts like this one. Ask each other questions about your likes and dislikes and write the answers on the chart.

	Rosana	Miguel	Ana	Elena	Yo
¿Te gusta el invierno?	No				
¿Te gusta estudiar?					
¿Te gusta la escuela?					
¿Te gusta ir al cine?					
¿Te gusta cantar?					

B Use your chart from the previous activity. Get together with a partner who was not in your group when you made the chart. Your partner asks you questions about the people on your chart, including yourself! Then switch roles.

MODELO —¿A Rosana le gusta el invierno?

—Sí, le gusta el invierno.
or No, no le gusta el invierno.

Entre amigos

Sit in a circle with three or four classmates. Everyone picks an activity that they like. (Make sure it's an activity you have learned how to say in Spanish!) Write yours secretly on a card.

The first person says his or her activity to the person sitting to his or her right, and asks if that person likes it. The second person answers according to his or her card.

—Me gusta patinar. ¿Te gusta patinar?
—No, no me gusta patinar. Me gusta cantar.
or Sí, me gusta patinar.

The second person does the same with the person to his or her right. Continue around the circle until everyone has had a chance to ask and answer. Then go around the circle saying what the person to your right likes.

—A Martín le gusta cantar.

CONEXIÓN CON LOS ESTUDIOS SOCIALES

World Travel You're a travel agent. Give advice to a partner about the best place to travel, according to his or her tastes. Ask questions such as **¿Te gusta el arte?, ¿Te gusta el sol?, ¿Te gusta la música?, ¿Te gusta el otoño?** and write the answers. Decide on the best destination for your partner.

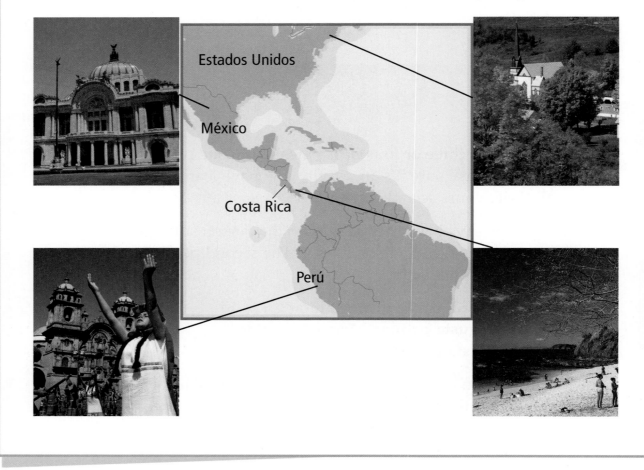

En resumen

		Me			pintar.
	(No)	Te	} gusta {		
(**A** Juan)		Le			el verano.

¿Cómo se dice?

Which one do you like?

When you use a descriptive word in English, it comes before the word it describes: *the blue house, the big bird.* But look where the descriptive words are placed in Spanish:

> No me gusta **el perro grande.**

> Me gusta **el triángulo verde.**

Do they come before or after the word they describe?

When you're describing things in English, you don't always say the name of the thing you're describing: *I like the blue one. Do you have the big one?* Here is how you do that in Spanish:

—¿Cuál te gusta, el bolígrafo rojo o el bolígrafo amarillo?

—Me gusta **el amarillo.**

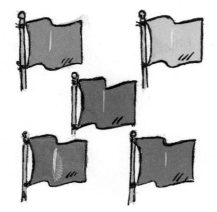

—¿Cuál te gusta, la bandera azul o la bandera verde?

—Me gusta **la verde.**

—¿Qué perro te gusta?

—Me gusta **el marrón.**

Do you see that you just use **el** or **la** and the descriptive word?

CONEXIÓN CON LA SALUD

Colors and Mood Studies show that colors can affect your mood. Here are some colors and the moods they help create. Look at the colors with a partner. Ask which of two colors your partner prefers because of the mood it creates.

MODELO —¿Qué color te gusta, el rojo o el azul?

—Me gusta el azul.

 soothes, promotes affection

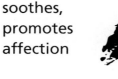 shows discipline, encourages independence

 balances, refreshes

cheers, increases energy

 cheers, stimulates appetite and conversation

 comforts, creates mystery

purifies, unifies

 empowering

 relaxes, cools, is peaceful

¡Úsalo!

A Get together with a partner. Tell each other which picture you prefer.

Partner A: Give your partner the choices.

Partner B: Answer according to your preference.

> **MODELO** —¿Cuál te gusta, el gato gris o el gato marrón?
>
> —Me gusta el marrón.

1.

2.

3.

4.

5.

6.

B You and your partner are at a school supply store. Make a list of things to buy. You mention an item and your partner asks which of two colors or sizes you prefer. Then your partner draws your preferences in your "shopping basket"—a sheet of paper! Then switch roles.

Partner A: Say an item from the list.

Partner B: Ask for a preference between two colors or sizes.

Partner A: Say your preference.

> **MODELO** —Un bolígrafo
>
> —¿Cuál te gusta, el negro o el azul?
>
> —Me gusta el azul.

CONEXIÓN CON EL ARTE

Animal Collage Make an animal collage! Find five different animal pictures in a magazine. Cut out or draw two of each, in different colors. Label your pictures. Your teacher will tell you the names of any animals you don't know. Make sure to write down whether the names use **el** or **la**.

Get together with a partner to decide which animals you will put in your collage.

> **MODELO** ¿Cuál te gusta, el azul o el verde?

Take turns picking animals for your collage.

Entre amigos

Play a game. Cut out squares of different colors—all the colors you've learned so far in Spanish.

Go up to a classmate. Without looking, pick two of your squares, hold them up, and ask your classmate **¿Cuál te gusta?** Your classmate answers **Me gusta (el verde).** Give your classmate the one he or she likes. Then your classmate asks the question using his or her color squares. You answer and your classmate gives you a color square. Do this with four more classmates.

Now put the color squares you've collected on your desk. Your teacher will name a color, for example **el azul.** Stand up if you have that color. Your teacher will name more colors. Sit down if you don't have the color named. If you do have that color, you should remain standing. Which colors are the most popular?

En resumen

¿Cuál te gusta?			Me gusta	el marrón.
¿Qué	**perro**	te gusta?		**la** amarilla.
	mariposa			

ciento treinta y cinco   **135**

¿Dónde se habla español?

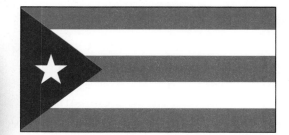

San Juan

PUERTO RICO

Puerto Rico

Puerto Rico is an island in the Caribbean. It is a mixture of three cultures: Spanish, African, and descendants of the indigenous population, **los taíno.** The Taínos called their island Borikén, or Borinquen, and the Spaniards renamed it Puerto Rico, which means "rich port." There is an interesting historical section in the capital, called **"el Viejo San Juan."** There are three forts there, all constructed during the Spanish colonization: **la Fortaleza, San Cristóbal** and **el Morro.** These forts were used to protect the city from pirates like Francis Drake, who roamed the seas looking to plunder ships that were returning to Spain full of gold, silver, and other valuable cargo. Look at Puerto Rico on the inset map and you'll understand its strategic location.

Puerto Rico has a mild climate all year round, so it's perfect for tourism and agriculture. Sugar cane and coffee are important crops. Bananas and their cousins, plantains, are also important exports. The plantains that Puerto Ricans don't export are often served fried. Prepared like this, they're called **tostones…** and they're **deliciosos!**

⊚⊚⊚⊚⊚ Datos ⊚⊚⊚⊚

Capital: San Juan

Ciudades importantes: Bayamón, Mayagüez, Ponce, Caguas

Idiomas: Español, inglés

Moneda: El dólar estadounidense

Población: 3.9 millones

El Yunque rain forest in Puerto Rico.

¡Léelo en español!

El Yunque La selva tropical[1] de El Yunque es un sitio fascinante de Puerto Rico. Si te gusta la naturaleza,[2] te va a gustar El Yunque. Es un refugio para animales, pájaros y muchas plantas. Un refugio es un sitio donde los animales y las plantas están bajo[3] la protección del gobierno.[4] En el Yunque vive el coquí. El coquí es el animal nacional de Puerto Rico y canta "co-quí, co-quí" constantemente. Es una rana muy pequeña. Hay también loros puertorriqueños en el refugio y muchas plantas tropicales, como las orquídeas.[5]

[1] rain forest   [2] nature   [3] are under
[4] government   [5] orchids

Reading Strategy

Reading Photo Captions
Before reading the selection, read the label under the photograph. This will give you a clue as to the topics covered in the reading. What topics will you find here?

¡Comprendo!

Complete each of the statements on a sheet of paper.

1. **El coquí** is _____.
   - **a.** a fort
   - **b.** a food
   - **c.** an animal
   - **d.** a plant

2. **El Morro** is a _____.
   - **a.** rain forest
   - **b.** plant
   - **c.** fort
   - **d.** pirate

3. **La orquídea** is a _____.
   - **a.** fort
   - **b.** food
   - **c.** dance
   - **d.** plant

4. **El Yunque** is a _____.
   - **a.** kind of frog
   - **b.** fort
   - **c.** rain forest
   - **d.** city

5. The national animal of Puerto Rico is _____.
   - **a.** el coquí
   - **b.** el loro
   - **c.** la orquídea
   - **d.** el refugio

UNIDAD 6

¿Cuándo es tu cumpleaños?

Día de San Juan celebration

Objetivos

- To learn the months of the year
- To talk about the things you like and don't like to do in different months
- To talk about who's doing something
- To talk about dates (like your birthday!)

FELIZ CUMPLEAÑOS

A girl prepares to swing at her birthday piñata.

¿Sabías que...?

- **Piñatas** are popular at birthday parties in many places in Latin America. They are full of fruit, candy, and other treats. Kids break them open with a stick, or pull from ribbons at the bottom to get a shower of treats!

- **Carnaval** is celebrated in February in many countries. People dress up in costumes. There are parades, music, and dancing everywhere.

Carnaval in Ponce, Puerto Rico

¿Cómo se dice?

What's the date?

—¿Qué fecha es hoy?

—Es el trece de enero.

enero

febrero

marzo

abril

mayo

junio

julio

agosto

septiembre

octubre

noviembre

diciembre

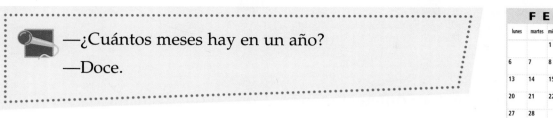

—¿Cuántos meses hay en un año?

—Doce.

un mes

FEBRERO

lunes	martes	miércoles	jueves	viernes	sábado	domingo
		1	2	3	4	5
6	7	8	9	10	11	12
13	14	15	16	17	18	19
20	21	22	23	24	25	26
27	28					

¿Cuándo es tu cumpleaños?

Es el doce de noviembre.

¿Sabías que...?

In Spanish, the first letter of each month is not capitalized. In dates, the day goes before the month.

CONEXIÓN CON LA CULTURA

Saint's Day For many people in Spanish-speaking countries, a person's "Saint's Day" **(día del santo)** is celebrated in addition to his or her birthday. Each saint has a special day during the year. The day for the saint that shares your name is your "Saint's Day." Here are some common **santos** and their dates. See if anyone you know has a **santo** on this list.

Joseph	José	19 de marzo
George	Jorge	23 de abril
John	Juan	24 de junio
Peter	Pedro	29 de junio
Paul	Pablo	29 de junio
Martha	Marta	29 de julio
Ellen	Elena	18 de agosto
Elizabeth	Isabel	5 de noviembre

¡Úsalo!

Make drawings that show four different months. Don't write the names of the months. Get together with two classmates and guess the months that they drew. Then they guess yours.

MODELO —¿Qué mes es?

—Es enero.

CONEXIÓN CON LAS MATEMÁTICAS

Addition Which month has the most birthdays? Survey your class, asking each classmate when his or her birthday is. Keep track on a chart like this one.

MODELO —¿Cuándo es tu cumpleaños?

—En enero.

Then add all your checkmarks and write the total in the third column. Get together with a partner and compare your results.

MODELO —En enero hay cuatro cumpleaños.

—Sí, y hay un cumpleaños en febrero.

—En marzo no hay cumpleaños.

Mes	Cumpleaños	Total
enero	✔✔✔✔	4
febrero	✔	1
marzo		0
abril		
mayo		
junio		
julio		
agosto		
septiembre		
octubre		
noviembre		
diciembre		

Entre amigos

Most people like to be wished a happy birthday. Your class is going to make a birthday list so you'll know everyone's birthday.

Pick a partner and ask the date of his or her birthday—in Spanish, of course! Your partner will answer, and then ask your birth date. Your teacher will write the names of the months on a list, and call out the names of each month. When your partner's birthday month is called, raise your hand and tell your partner's name and birthday.

El cumpleaños de Marcos es el primero de octubre.

Your teacher will put the list in a place where everyone can see it. Check the list every day to see if someone has a birthday. Be sure to wish them . . .

¡Feliz cumpleaños!

En resumen

un mes

¿Qué fecha **es** hoy?
    Es el trece de enero.
                    febrero.
                    marzo.
                    abril.
                    mayo.
                    junio.
                    julio.
                    agosto.
                    septiembre.
                    octubre.
                    noviembre.
                    diciembre.

¿Cuándo **es** tu cumpleaños?
    Es el doce de noviembre.

¿Cómo se dice?

What do you like to do?

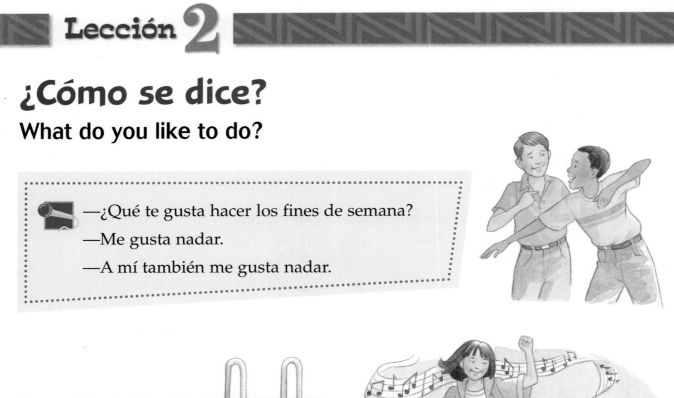

—¿Qué te gusta hacer los fines de semana?

—Me gusta nadar.

—A mí también me gusta nadar.

nadar

bailar

caminar

patinar

—No me gusta limpiar.
—A mí tampoco.

comprar **limpiar** **dibujar** **jugar**

CONEXIÓN CON LA CULTURA

Traditional Games Children in Spanish-speaking countries like to play many traditional games. In Colombia, children get in line and hold on to the waist or shoulders of the person in front of them. The first person in line tries to catch the last person in line. The other children try to avoid this by moving the line around! The game is called **la culebra** *(the snake)*. Why do you think it has this name?

¡Úsalo!

A Ask your partner what he or she likes to do. Then your partner will ask you the same questions.

Partner A: Ask your partner if he or she likes doing the activity pictured.

Partner B: Answer according to what you like or don't like to do.

MODELO —¿Te gusta caminar?

—Sí, me gusta caminar. *or* No, no me gusta caminar.

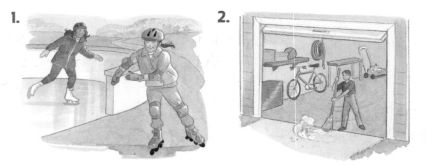

B Make a chart like this one. Write the activities that you like and dislike doing in different seasons.

Now tell your partner what you like and dislike doing in each season.

	Me gusta...	No me gusta...
primavera	caminar	patinar
verano		
otoño		
invierno		

MODELO —En primavera, me gusta caminar. No me gusta patinar.

C Work with a partner. Think of all the activities you've learned to say in Spanish. Mention three that you like doing and three that you don't like doing. Your partner will tell you if he or she likes or dislikes the same things. Then switch roles.

MODELO —Me gusta practicar deportes.

—A mí también. *or* No me gusta.

—No me gusta cantar.

—A mí tampoco. *or* A mí me gusta.

¿Sabías que...?

On the night of June 23, people in many countries celebrate the arrival of summer—the **Día de San Juan.** In some places, like Spain and Puerto Rico, people light bonfires on the beach and take a midnight dip in the ocean for good luck.

CONEXIÓN CON EL ARTE

Collage Make a class calendar collage! Work together with two classmates. Your teacher will ask one of you to pick a card with the month for your calendar.

Draw the following things, or cut them out of a magazine or newspaper. Make sure the words are in Spanish!

- the name of the month
- the days of the week
- numbers from 1 to 31
- four or five things that remind you of that month
- four or five things that you like to do in that month

Then divide a piece of posterboard in half. Make a collage on the top half from the pictures you've collected. Make a grid for the calendar on the bottom. Write in the days of the week and the correct numbers for your month.

Now you and your classmates have a calendar you can use all year long!

JULIO

domingo	lunes	martes	miércoles	jueves	viernes	sábado
				1	2	3
4	5	6	7	8	9	10
11	12	13	14	15	16	17
18	19	20	21	22	23	24
25	26	27	28	29	30	31

En resumen

¿Qué **te gusta** hacer los fines de semana?
en el verano?

Me gusta bailar.
caminar.
comprar.
dibujar.
jugar.
limpiar.
nadar.
patinar.

Me gusta nadar.   **No me gusta** bailar.
A mí **también.**   A mí **tampoco.**

¿Cómo se dice?

Who's doing what?

Study the sentence with each picture. Which word tells you who is painting?

¿Quién pinta?

Yo pinto.

Tú pintas.

Él pinta.

Ella pinta.

In English, to say who is doing something, you can use the person's name or you can substitute a word like *I, you, he,* or *she.* These words are pronouns. You can do the same thing in Spanish with the words **yo, tú, él,** and **ella.**

But many times in Spanish, you can leave these words out.

—¿Nadas mucho?

—Sí. Nado los sábados y los domingos.

You only need to use the person's name or a pronoun if it's not clear whom you're talking about or if you want to emphasize who is doing what.

—¿Quién pinta, María o Pablo?

—*Él* pinta.

—¿Quién nada, tú o Juan?

—*Yo* nado.

CONEXIÓN CON LA SALUD

Fitness Chart You know that it's important to keep active and exercise often. Think of activities you would like to do in the next two weeks to stay fit. Make a chart like this one and write in these activities.

practicar deportes		nadar		caminar		bailar		patinar

lunes	martes	miércoles	jueves	viernes	sábado	domingo

Then get together with a partner and tell him or her what you will do in the next two weeks.

MODELO Voy a nadar el viernes.

Exchange charts with your partner. When your teacher asks **¿Quién nada?**, answer with your partner's name: **(Laura) nada.**

¡Úsalo!

A Ask your partner if he or she does the following activities. Then switch roles.

MODELO —¿Bailas?

—Sí, bailo. *or* No, no bailo.

1.

2.

3.

4.

5.

6.

B Draw three of the activities listed below on different cards. Then get together with three or four classmates. Shuffle all the cards and put them facedown in a pile. Take turns picking out three cards. Then one of you asks who does a certain activity, for example, **¿Quién baila?** Everyone takes a turn answering, according to the cards that he or she has.

nadar	bailar	caminar	patinar
comprar	limpiar	dibujar	

MODELO —¿Quién baila?

—Yo bailo.

—Yo también bailo.

—Yo no bailo.

—Yo tampoco.

C Use the cards from Activity B. Sit in a circle with four classmates. The first person shows one card and says that he or she does that activity, for example: **Yo limpio.** The second person shows one of his or her cards and adds to the first sentence: **Alicia limpia y yo estudio.** Go once around the circle saying everyone's activities and adding your own. Then start over, but have another person go first.

MODELO —**Alicia limpia, Raúl estudia y yo trabajo.**

En resumen

	pintar	nadar	bailar	caminar	patinar	*endings*
	pint-	nad-	bail-	camin-	patin-	
yo	pinto	nado	bailo	camino	patino	**-o**
tú	pintas	nadas	bailas	caminas	patinas	**-as**
él, ella	pinta	nada	baila	camina	patina	**-a**

Entre amigos

Make a chart like this one. Then work with two classmates to find out more about them. Ask them the questions on the chart and write the name of the classmate who does each activity.

—¿Quién baila bien?

—Yo bailo bien.

—Yo no. *or* Yo también.

	¿Quién?
¿Quién baila bien?	Marisa, Olga
¿Quién limpia en casa?	
¿Quién camina en el parque?	
¿Quién patina en invierno?	Marisa
¿Quién dibuja bien?	
¿Quién estudia mucho?	
¿Quién nada en verano?	

Then get together with two different classmates. Tell them what you have learned, without saying any names. They have to guess who you're talking about.

—Baila bien y patina en invierno.

—¿Es Marisa?

Lección 4

¿Cómo se dice?

Describing how often you do something

Do you always swim in June? Or sometimes walk to school in the spring? Perhaps you never skate, not even in the winter. Look at Daniel's schedules to see how to say things like these in Spanish.

L	M	M	J	V	S	D
✓	✓	✓	✓	✓	✓	✓
✓	✓	✓	✓	✓	✓	✓

L	M	M	J	V	S	D
✓			✓			
	✓	✓				✓

L	M	M	J	V	S	D

Daniel **siempre** estudia en la casa.

Daniel **a veces** camina a la tienda.

Daniel **nunca** patina.

¡Úsalo!

A Interview a partner to find out how often he or she does some activities. Make a chart like this one. Put a check mark in the correct box to show his or her answer.

> **MODELO** —¿Nadas en verano?
>
> —Nunca nado en verano.

	siempre	a veces	nunca
¿Nadas en invierno?	✔	☐	☐
¿Bailas los fines de semana?	☐	☐	☐
¿Caminas en el parque?	☐	✔	☐
¿Patinas en invierno?	☐	☐	☐
¿Compras en las tiendas?	☐	☐	☐
¿Dibujas en el salón de clase?	☐	☐	☐

After the interview, write a paragraph about your partner's activities.

¿Sabías que...?

In Spain, school starts at nine in the morning. Many children go home for lunch at one. They return to school at three and stay in school until five in the afternoon. They often do sports or other after-school activities, and return home around seven. How does their school day compare to yours?

B Write questions about the following activities to ask your partner. Use words from the two boxes.

bailar
nadar
estudiar
usar la computadora
patinar
limpiar
practicar deportes

en agosto
en invierno
en la escuela
en el parque
en la casa
los domingos
en el salón de clase

Ask your partner your questions. Your partner answers whether he or she does these activities sometimes, always, or never.

MODELO —¿Bailas en la escuela?

—No, nunca bailo en la escuela.
or Sí, siempre bailo en la escuela.
or A veces bailo en la escuela.

CONEXIÓN CON LAS CIENCIAS

The Weather What's the weather like where you live? Talk with your partner about the weather events that always, never, and sometimes happen in each season. Then write sentences about the weather. Use the weather expressions you know.

MODELO En verano nunca llueve.

Entre amigos

Birthdays and **santos** are just two of the days that people celebrate. Look at this list of different **días de fiesta**:

Año Nuevo	**1 de enero**
Día del Amor y la Amistad	**14 de febrero**
Día de San Patricio	**17 de marzo**
Día de la Madre	**en el mes de mayo**
Día del Padre	**en el mes de junio**
Día de la Independencia (EE. UU.)	**4 de julio**
Día de los Veteranos	**11 de noviembre**
Día de Acción de Gracias	**en el mes de noviembre**

Get together with a partner. Take turns picking different holidays. Say when the holiday is, and ask each other if you ever celebrate **(celebrar)** the holiday.

> —**El día de San Patricio es el diecisiete de marzo. ¿Celebras tú el día de San Patricio?**
>
> —**Sí, a veces. ¿Y tú?**
>
> —**No, yo nunca celebro el día de San Patricio.**

En resumen

Daniel **siempre** estudia en la casa.
Daniel **a veces** camina a la tienda.
Daniel **nunca** patina.

¿Dónde se habla español?
Puerto Rican Music

Puerto Rican music is strongly influenced by African culture. **La bomba** is a Puerto Rican dance derived from slaves brought to the island from West Africa. In **la bomba,** a dialogue takes place between the drummers and the dancer. It was sung by enslaved Africans to ease the hardships of slavery. **La plena** is a dance that also came from enslaved Africans. It uses a number of musical instruments such as **el cuatro** (pictured at right), an instrument derived from the Spanish guitar; **el güiro,** which originated from the Taínos; and **los panderos** which evolved from Spanish tambourines. **La salsa** is a more modern dance and form of music that originated among Puerto Ricans living in Spanish Harlem, New York. Salsa is also strongly influenced by African rhythms.

Datos

A.D.1000: The first inhabitants of Puerto Rico are the Taínos. They call the island Borikén.

1493: Christopher Columbus arrives in Puerto Rico on November 19 during his second voyage.

1509: The Spanish crown allows Spaniards to use the Taínos for wage-free and forced labor in the gold mines. In a couple of years, the Taíno population is devastated.

1513: Enslaved Africans are brought to the island to replace the Taínos in the gold mines.

1736: Large plantations are established to increase sugarcane production using enslaved Africans.

1868: An uprising against Spanish rule takes place—**El Grito de Lares** (*The Cry of Lares*). It is suppressed by the Spanish government.

1897: Spain grants Puerto Rico autonomy.

1898: Upon winning the Spanish-American War, the United States takes possession of Puerto Rico, Cuba, and the Philippines from Spain under the Treaty of Paris.

1917: Puerto Ricans are declared U.S. citizens.

1952: Puerto Rico becomes a Commonwealth of the United States.

¡Léelo en español!

La artesanía[1] tradicional Las máscaras son de origen africano y español. Muchas personas usan máscaras durante el Carnaval. En Ponce, el Carnaval es en febrero. Los niños y adultos usan las máscaras y disfraces[2] de muchos colores. Las artesanías de los Tres Reyes Magos[3] son de origen español. Hay todo tipo[4] de artesanías de Reyes Magos. Son muy populares en invierno. El Día de los Reyes es el 6 de enero.

[1] crafts   [2] costumes   [3] Three Kings   [4] all sorts

Making Comparisons Think about any traditional crafts that you're familiar with. Comparing these to the topics you're going to read about will make your reading task easier.

Recognizing Cognates What do you think these words mean: **tradicional, máscaras, origen, africano, personas, Carnaval, adultos, populares?** Use these cognates to help you understand what is being said about Puerto Rican crafts.

¡Comprendo!

Answer in English.

1. Why were enslaved Africans brought to Puerto Rico?

2. What did the United States gain during the Spanish-American war?

3. What three cultures influenced Puerto Rican music and crafts?

4. What three dances are popular in Puerto Rico?

5. What are two traditional crafts found in Puerto Rico?

7

¿Cómo estás?

Objetivos

- To talk about how you are feeling and ask others about their feelings
- To tell your age and ask about the age of others
- To learn when to use **tú** and when to use **usted**

An arrival and departure schedule board at an airport

A woman quenches her thirst with a drink of water

Twin girls celebrate their **quinceañera**

¿Sabías que...?

- Not everyone in the Spanish-speaking world uses the same words for certain things. In Argentina and in some other countries, people use the word **vos** instead of **tú,** and they use different verb endings, too!

- In many Spanish-speaking countries, people have more vacation days than in the United States. Traditionally, some businesses in Spain closed in August, but this is changing. Other businesses have summer hours that allow workers to start around nine and leave for the day around two.

¿Cómo se dice?

What's the matter?

—¿Qué tienes?

—Tengo frío.

Tengo frío.

Tengo calor.

Tengo sed.

Tengo hambre.

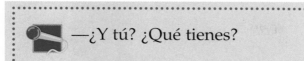

—¿Y tú? ¿Qué tienes?

Tengo sueño.

Tengo la gripe.

Tengo miedo.

CONEXIÓN CON LA CULTURA

Siesta Time Are you ever tired after a big lunch? A lot of people are! In some Spanish-speaking countries, many businesses close from about noon until 3:00 p.m. every day. This long break is called **la siesta,** and for many years people would use this time to take a nap after lunch and before returning to work. Now most people use this break just to take a long lunch and relax. In some cities, however, this custom is changing or disappearing because of the faster pace of today's business world.

¡Úsalo!

Get together with a partner. Take turns asking each other questions based on the pictures.

MODELO —¿Tienes frío?

—No, no tengo frío.

CONEXIÓN CON LAS CIENCIAS

Temperature Work with a partner and take turns reading out loud the temperatures on these thermometers. Then ask your partner whether he or she is hot or cold, according to the temperatures. Make sure to say the temperature in both scales—Fahrenheit and Celsius!

MODELO —Son sesenta y ocho grados Fahrenheit. Son veinte grados Celsius.

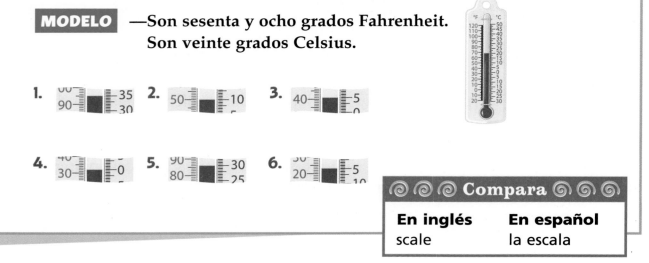

@@@ **Compara** @@@

En inglés	En español
scale	la escala

Entre amigos

Form a group with three or four classmates. Use index cards and colored pencils or markers to draw pictures or symbols that show the seven different situations on pages 162–163.

Put the cards facedown in a pile. Draw a card, but don't show it to the other players. The rest of your group must take turns asking questions to find out what's on your card.

—¿Tienes sueño?
—No, no tengo sueño.
—¿Tienes miedo?
—No, no tengo miedo.
—¿Tienes sed?
—Sí. Tengo sed.

When someone guesses correctly, show your card to the group, then return it to the bottom of the pile. The person who guessed correctly gets to pick the next card, and the game continues. Play until your teacher calls time.

En resumen

¿Qué **tienes?**
   Tengo calor.
            frío.
            la gripe.
            hambre.
            miedo.
            sed.
            sueño.
¿Y tú?

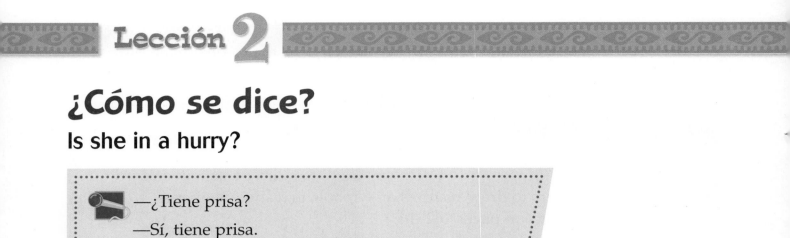

Lección 2

¿Cómo se dice?

Is she in a hurry?

—¿Tiene prisa?

—Sí, tiene prisa.

Tiene prisa.

un pizarrón

Tiene razón.

Tiene suerte.

—¿Cuántos años tiene?

—Tiene ochenta años. Hoy es su cumpleaños.

Tiene ochenta años.

CONEXIÓN CON LA CULTURA

In Spanish-speaking countries, when a girl turns fifteen, it's customary for her family to throw a big party and invite all their friends and relatives. She's called a **quinceañera.** She wears a special dress for her quinceañera and celebrates becoming a young woman.

¡Úsalo!

A Get together with a partner and decide on the best way to describe each situation. Choose from these expressions.

Tiene suerte.	No tiene suerte.	Tiene prisa.
No tiene prisa.	Tiene miedo.	No tiene miedo.
Tiene razón.	No tiene razón.	

1.

2.

3.

4.

5.

6.

B Everyone thinks they're right, but they're not! Who's right in each picture? Get together with a partner. Take turns asking and answering who is right.

MODELO —¿Quién tiene razón?

1.
Isabel: Es rojo.
Pedro: Es negro.
Claudia: Es blanco.
Mateo: Es azul.

2.
Miguel: Hace calor.
Rosa: Hace viento.
José: Llueve.
María: Nieva.

3.
Pepe: Es gordo.
Ana: Es alto.
Carlos: Es grande.
Manuel: Es pequeño.

4.
Lina: Es un mapa.
Pablo: Es una papelera.
Luisa: Es un pizarrón.
Lucas: Es una computadora.

En resumen

¿**Tiene** prisa?	¿Cuántos años **tiene?**
Sí, **tiene** prisa. razón. suerte.	**Tiene** ochenta años.

Lección 3

¿Cómo se dice?

Talking with classmates and adults

In English, when you talk to someone, you use only one word—"you."
In Spanish there are two ways to say "you." Look carefully at the people
in the pictures and read the sentences. Which word is used for "you"?

Tú bailas muy bien.

Tú nadas muy bien.

Tú cantas muy bien.

Now study these pictures and sentences. Which word is used for "you"?

Usted baila muy bien.

Usted nada muy bien.

Usted canta muy bien.

Can you see the difference between **tú** and **usted**? Use **tú** with other kids,
as well as with family members. Use **usted** with everyone else.

Did you also notice that the verb forms change, too? These verbs end in **–as** with **tú** and in **–a** with **usted.**

¿Cómo te llamas?

Señor, ¿cómo se llama?

Notice that many times, Spanish speakers skip the words **tú** or **usted** when they are talking to the person. This is because the ending of the verb, **–as** or **–a,** tells the listener which word for "you" is being used!

¿Sabías que...?

In some countries, the use of **usted** is more common than in others. In Colombia, even parents and children may use **usted** among themselves! To know whether you would call someone **usted,** think of whether you would say *Mr., Miss, Ms.,* or *Mrs.* before that person's name. In English, it's one way of showing politeness to people older than you or to people you don't know.

¡Úsalo!

A Look at the following pictures and write or say whether you would use **tú** or **usted** to speak to each person. Then complete the sentence with the correct form of the verb in parentheses.

> **MODELO** _____ (tener) frío.
>
> —**Usted tiene frío.**

1. _____ (usar) la computadora los fines de semana.

2. _____ (estudiar) mucho.

3. _____ nunca (bailar).

4. ¿Cuándo _____ (practicar) deportes?

5. No _____ (tener) miedo.

B Get together with a partner and look at this conversation between a student and a teacher. Make up the missing parts of the conversation, using the correct forms for **tú** and **usted.** Write them on a sheet of paper, and then act them out with your partner.

C A group of students and teachers from South America is visiting your school, and you want to ask them some questions. Say or write which question you'd ask each of them.

1. Alejandro Peña

   a. ¿Cómo está usted?

   b. ¿Cómo estás tú?

2. Señorita Cortez

   a. ¿Usa la computadora?

   b. ¿Usas la computadora?

3. María Elena Solís

   a. ¿Vas tú a la clase de música?

   b. ¿Va usted a la clase de música?

4. Señora Vásquez

   a. ¿Qué haces tú en agosto?

   b. ¿Qué hace usted en agosto?

Entre amigos

Think of the names of two different people who are known to everyone in the class. They can be teachers, other students, or celebrities. Try to include people of different ages. Write each name on a separate card. Use complete names and titles such as **Doctora** or **Señor,** if appropriate.

Put all the names in a bag. Pass the bag around the class and take turns drawing one card at a time. Read the name aloud and make up one sentence or question that you would use if you met that person.

Señor Antonio Banderas
—¿Usted usa mucho la computadora?

En resumen

(Tú) Bail**as** muy bien.
¿Cómo te llam**as?**

(Usted) Bail**a** muy bien.
¿Cómo se llam**a?**

¿Cómo se dice?

Saying what you have and how you are

Sometimes you use the verb **tener** to talk about "having something."
Look at these sentences.

Tengo dos libros.

¿Tienes un globo?

Sara **tiene** una computadora.

You can also use **tener** to talk about how you are or how you feel.

Tengo calor.

¿Tienes calor?

¿Tiene usted calor?

Él **tiene** calor.

Ella **tiene** calor.

Did you notice how **tener** changes depending on which person it is used with? If you use it to talk about yourself, the form is **tengo.** When you're talking to a friend, it's **tienes,** and with adults whom you call **usted,** it's **tiene.** Also, when you're talking about another person, it's **tiene.**

These different forms are used even if you don't actually say or write the words **yo, tú, usted, él,** or **ella.**

CONEXIÓN CON LAS MATEMÁTICAS

Probability Test your luck. With a partner, put three identical marbles of different colors in a bag. Mix them up and reach into the bag. How many times do you think you will pick out the red one?

Make a guess and then do an experiment. Keep picking a marble and putting it back. Repeat this 30 times. Count how many times you get each color.

Rojo	✓
Azul	
Amarillo	

Compare your results with other pairs. Who was luckier at getting closest to his or her guess? What do you think would happen if you repeated the experiment 100 times?

¡Úsalo!

A Draw and color animals you know on four different cards. You can draw one or more on each card. Get together with a partner. Take turns asking each other about the animals you each have. Write a description of your partner's animals.

> **MODELO** —¿Qué tienes?
>
> —Tengo un gato gris.

Find a new partner. Tell him or her the animals your old partner has.

> **MODELO** —Isabel tiene un gato gris, cuatro mariposas azules, dos perros negros y tres canarios amarillos.

B Play a game show with a partner. For every answer that your partner gives you, ask a corresponding question.

> **MODELO** —La señora Prado tiene sesenta y tres años.
>
> —¿Cuántos años tiene la señora Prado?

1. Sí, Humberto tiene frío.
2. No, Amalia no tiene hambre.
3. Sí, tengo mucha sed.
4. Tengo cincuenta años.
5. No, Sandra no tiene sueño.
6. Sí, tengo prisa.
7. Tienes nueve años.
8. Sí, Mercedes tiene razón.
9. No, Rogelio no tiene la gripe.
10. No, el señor Ortiz no tiene suerte.

C You want to find out more about your partner. Make a chart like this one and ask questions about how often he or she feels this way.

	siempre ●	a veces ◐	nunca ○
frío			
calor			
suerte			
sed			
hambre			
miedo			
la gripe			
sueño			

Then switch partners. Tell your new partner about your first partner.

MODELO —David siempre tiene frío, nunca tiene calor, a veces tiene suerte, siempre tiene sed, siempre tiene hambre y nunca tiene sueño. A veces tiene miedo y nunca tiene la gripe.

CONEXIÓN CON LA SALUD

Based on the information you gave your partners, decide how you can change your habits to be more healthful. Choose the answers that you do not think are healthful. Draw some tips about what you can do to improve your habits.

Entre amigos

It's acting time! Your teacher will give you a card with an expression using **tener.** When it's your turn, you have to act out the expression on your card.

Your classmates will ask you about how you feel or what you have **(¿Tienes miedo? ¿Tienes dos perros?).** The first one to guess your expression gets to go next.

Keep track of the expressions that each person acts out. When your teacher asks about how someone feels or what he or she has, you'll be able to answer!

Tomás—frío
Raquel—hambre
Jaime—dos libros

Tengo miedo.

Tengo 9 años.

En resumen

(yo)	**Tengo** dos libros.	¿**Tengo** (yo) el libro?
(tú)	**Tienes** un globo.	¿**Tienes** (tú) calor?
(él)		¿**Tiene** (él, ella, usted) un
(ella) }	**Tiene** calor.	lápiz?
(usted)		

¿Dónde se habla español?

Ecuador

Ecuador is named for the equator that passes through it. Stone Age dwellers lived here as early as 9,000 B.C. Later the country became part of the great Incan empire. The Andes Mountains cut through Ecuador from north to south and Quito, situated at more than two miles above sea level, is the second highest capital in the world.

The world's highest active volcano in the world, Cotopaxi, is only a short drive from the capital. Open-air markets are especially popular in small towns, where villagers meet to socialize, as well as to trade their goods. The market in the town of Otavalo is well known for the handicrafts the villagers sell; blankets, sweaters, rugs, and belts are just a few of the items you can find there.

◎ ◎ ◎ ◎ Datos ◎ ◎ ◎ ◎

Capital: Quito

Ciudades importantes: Guayaquil, Cuenca, Riobamba

Idiomas: Español, quechua, jarvo

Moneda: El dólar estadounidense

Población: 13.7 millones

¡Léelo en español!

Las islas Galápagos Las islas Galápagos son de Ecuador. Están en el océano Pacifico, a 600 millas de la costa ecuatoriana. Hay trece islas principales, ocho islas más pequeñas y 40 islitas. Muchas personas quieren[1] visitar las islas para ver[2] la gran diversidad de las especies. Pero el gobierno controla las visitas para proteger[3] los animales, pájaros y plantas. No vas a las islas para tomar el sol.[4] Vas a las islas para observar. Hay tortugas gigantes. Las tortugas gigantes pueden vivir[5] 150 años. Hay iguanas. También hay muchos pájaros como los pingüinos blancos y negros y los piqueros de patas azules[6].

[1] want   [2] in order to see   [3] in order to protect
[4] to sunbathe   [5] can live   [6] blue-footed boobies

Reading Strategy

Skimming List three things that you would expect to find in a reading about the Galapagos Islands. Then skim the paragraph to find the information.

Recognizing Cognates What do you think these words mean: **costa, principales, diversidad, especies, gigantes?** Use these cognates to help you understand what is being said about Ecuador.

¡Comprendo!

Answer these questions on a sheet of paper.

1. Where are **las islas Galápagos?**

2. Name four of the animals that live there.

3. Why do you think some of the animals need to be protected?

8

¿Qué hora es?

Objetivos

- To ask and tell what time it is
- To say at what time you do different things
- To talk about how much time someone spends doing something
- To say how many minutes are in different lengths of time

The Paine Massif at sunrise, Torres de Paine National Park, Chile

Ancient sundial at
Machu Picchu, Peru

Ready, set, go!

¿Sabías que...?

- The ancient Mayans of Mexico used the sun, shadows, and stars to tell time. Their "clocks" kept time very accurately. Some of their calendars were more precise than the one used now.

- It takes only months to build a modern house. But some of the great castles and cathedrals in Spain took hundreds of years to build.

- In many Spanish-speaking countries, the 24-hour clock is used in schedules. In this system, 1:00 p.m. is 13 h, and midnight is 24 h. In the United States, we call this "military time."

¿Cómo se dice?

How much time is there?

—¿Cuántos minutos hay en un cuarto de hora?

—Hay quince minutos en un cuarto de hora.

un minuto

un cuarto de hora

media hora

una hora

una hora y cuarto

una hora y media

—¿Cuántas horas hay en un día?

—Hay veinticuatro horas en un día.

CONEXIÓN CON LAS MATEMÁTICAS

Amounts of Time
Multiply and/or add to find the number of minutes in each of the following. Write or say your answers.

¿Cuántos minutos hay?

un cuarto de hora + doce minutos   = _____ minutos

una hora y cuarto   = _____ minutos

una media hora + veinticuatro   = _____ minutos

una hora y media   = _____ minutos

tres cuartos de hora   = _____ minutos

◎ ◎ ◎ Compara ◎ ◎ ◎

En inglés	En español
hour	la hora
minute	el minuto
quarter	el cuarto

¿Sabías que...?

The meaning of "on time" varies from culture to culture. In some cultures, punctuality is very important. In others, people are more relaxed about punctuality. For example, in Spain people tend to arrive for events at the precise time. In Guatemala, "on time" **(a tiempo)** can mean within half an hour or more of the scheduled time. In Mexico, if you are **a tiempo** for a party starting at 8:00, you might not arrive until 10:00. People often refer to this idea of time as **la hora latina.** How is this different from the culture in the United States?

¡Úsalo!

A Susana made a chart showing what she's going to do each day after school. Her chart has clocks that help her see how much time (**tiempo**) she'll spend doing each activity. Read Susana's chart together with a partner and take turns asking and answering the questions.

> **MODELO** —¿Cuánto tiempo va a nadar Susana?
>
> —Va a nadar una hora.

1. ¿Cuánto tiempo va a practicar deportes Susana?

2. ¿Cuánto tiempo va a estudiar Susana?

3. ¿Cuánto tiempo va a caminar Susana?

4. ¿Cuánto tiempo va a cantar Susana?

5. ¿Cuánto tiempo va a usar la computadora Susana?

Actividad	Tiempo
Voy a practicar deportes.	
Voy a cantar.	
Voy a caminar.	
Voy a estudiar.	
Voy a nadar.	
Voy a usar la computadora.	

B Make your own chart like Susana's. Choose five things you're going to do today or tomorrow and write a sentence for each one. Next to each sentence, draw a clock or clocks to show how long you plan to do that activity.

MODELO **Voy a patinar.**

Now, get together with a partner and ask each other questions about your charts.

MODELO —**¿Qué vas a hacer mañana?**
—**Voy a patinar.**
—**¿Cuánto tiempo vas a patinar?**
—**Voy a patinar media hora.**

CONEXIÓN CON LAS MATEMÁTICAS

Measuring Time Work with a partner to decide if these periods of time or events are best measured in minutes, hours, days, months, weeks, or years.

una hora	**los días de la semana**	**estudiar en la biblioteca**
un cumpleaños	**los meses del año**	**el fin de semana**
la primavera	**la clase de arte**	**el verano**

En resumen

un minuto
el tiempo

¿Cuántos minutos **hay** en un cuarto de hora?
media hora?
una hora?
una hora y cuarto?
una hora y media?

¿Cómo se dice?

What time of the day is it?

—¿Cuándo vas a la biblioteca?

—Voy por la tarde.

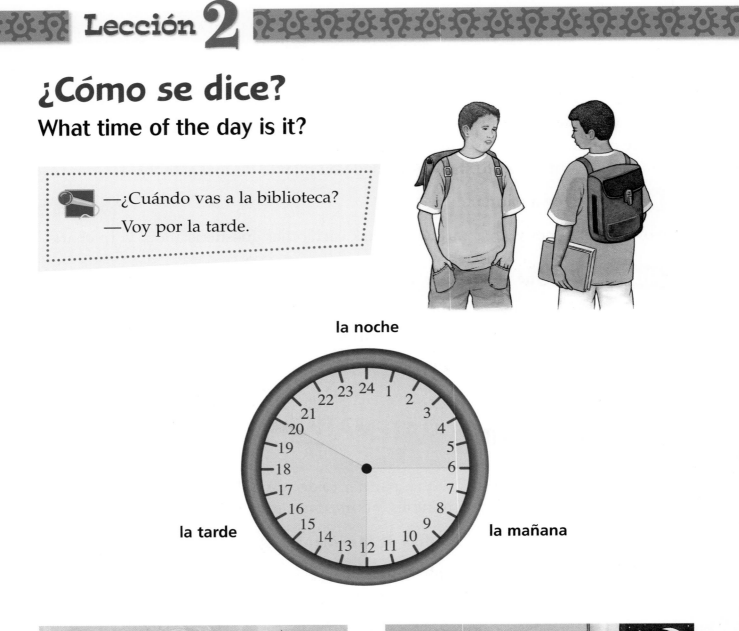

la noche

la tarde

la mañana

el mediodía

la medianoche

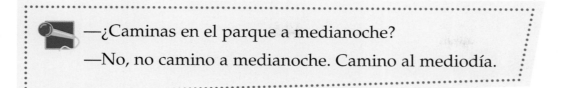

—¿Caminas en el parque a medianoche?

—No, no camino a medianoche. Camino al mediodía.

la salida del sol

la puesta del sol

CONEXIÓN CON LAS CIENCIAS

The Spanish Empire The Spanish empire was sometimes said to be an empire "where the sun never set." Look at the map below. It shows all the regions that used to be part of the Spanish empire. Why do you think it was said that the sun never set on Spain's empire?

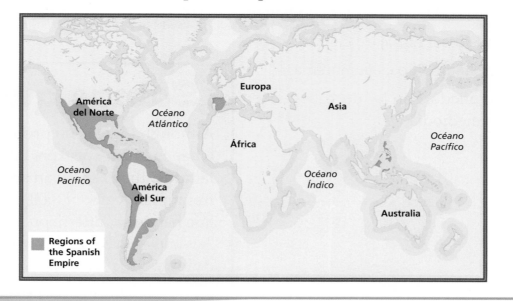

¡Úsalo!

A Get together with a partner. Take turns asking and answering what time of day goes best with the sentences below. You can use a time of day more than once. Some sentences may have more than one answer.

a. la puesta del sol

b. la salida del sol

c. el mediodía

d. la tarde

e. la noche

f. la medianoche

g. la mañana

> **MODELO** —Tengo frío. No hace sol. No es la tarde. ¿Cuándo es?
> —Es medianoche.

1. ¡Tengo prisa! Camino a la escuela.

2. No es la mañana. Sara tiene hambre. Hace mucho sol.

3. ¡Buenas noches! Tengo mucho sueño. No hace sol.

4. Voy a casa. Voy a estudiar. No hay mucho sol.

5. ¡Buenos días! El pájaro canta.

6. Tienes sueño. No es la mañana.

7. Tengo miedo. Son las doce. No es mediodía.

¿Sabías que...?

Although there is no precise rule, when Spanish-speakers talk about **la tarde,** they can mean anywhere from noon to about 8:00 p. m. The line between "afternoon" and "evening" in Spanish varies by country.

B Write in Spanish three different things you do. Then, write the time of day when you do these three things, for example: **Bailo—por la noche.**

Form a circle with three or four classmates. One person starts by saying something he or she does **(Bailo.).** The rest of the group tries to guess when the activity takes place **(por la mañana, por la tarde, por la noche).** The first person responds according to what he or she wrote.

MODELO —**Bailo.**

—**¿Bailas por la tarde?**

—**No, no bailo por la tarde. Bailo por la noche.**

CONEXIÓN CON LOS ESTUDIOS SOCIALES

Sunrise and Sunset As you know, the sun rises in the east and sets in the west. Look at the sun and say whether each picture shows **la mañana, la tarde,** or **el mediodía.**

En resumen

¿Cuándo **vas** a la biblioteca?
   Voy por la mañana.
       por la tarde.
       por la noche.
       al mediodía.
       a medianoche.

la salida del sol
la puesta del sol

¿Cómo se dice?

What time is it?

Look at these sentences to see how you can answer the question **¿Qué hora es?**

Es la una.

Son las dos.

Es la una y veinte.

Son las siete y cuarto.

Son las seis y media.

You use **es** with **la una** and times that include **la una,** and you use **son** with all other times or hours.

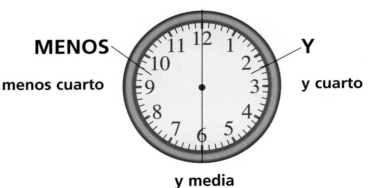

mediodía / medianoche

MENOS

menos cuarto

Y

y cuarto

y media

Use **menos** when the time is between the half hour and the next hour on the clock.

Es la una
menos cuarto.

Son las siete
menos veintitrés.

Son las cuatro
menos diez.

When you use **menos** you are subtracting the number of minutes between the number 12 and the minute hand. It's similar to what you say in English: "It's twenty to twelve." or "It's twenty of twelve."

These sentences show you how to say it is exactly a certain time and what time and part of day it is.

¡Es la una **en punto!**

Son las siete **de la mañana.**

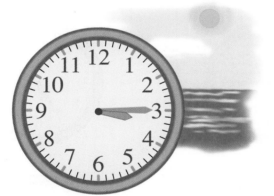

Son las tres y cuarto **de la tarde.**

Son las nueve menos diez **de la noche.**

To ask when people are going to do different things, you can use **¿A qué hora... ?** or **¿Cuándo... ?**

—**¿A qué hora** vas a la escuela?
—Voy **a** las ocho menos veinte de la mañana.

—**¿Cuándo** vas a la clase de música?
—Voy a la clase de música **a** las dos menos cuarto de la tarde.

When you answer questions about time, be sure to use the word **a** before the time.

¡Úsalo!

A Get together with a partner. Tell your partner the time on each clock. Your partner writes it down in numbers. When you finish, your partner reads the times back to you to check his or her answers.

MODELO —Son las siete y cuarto.

7:15

1.

2.

3.
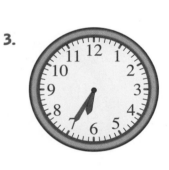

4.

5.

6.

7.

8.

9.

B Verónica and Víctor are very busy twins. Their mother has to post their Saturday schedules on the refrigerator! Talk with a partner about their schedules.

Partner A: Ask the questions about the twins' schedules.

Partner B: Answer according to the schedule.

> **MODELO** —¿A qué hora va él al cine?
>
> —Él va al cine a las siete y cinco de la tarde.

1. ¿A qué hora va ella a la clase de música?
2. ¿A qué hora va él a la clase de computadoras?
3. ¿Cuándo va ella a la biblioteca?
4. ¿Cuándo va él a la clase de arte?
5. ¿Cuándo va ella a la casa de la señora Millán?
6. ¿Cuándo va ella al cine?
7. ¿A qué hora va él al gimnasio?

	Verónica		Víctor	
8:30 a.m.	la clase de música	9:00 a.m.	el gimnasio
10:45 a.m.	la biblioteca	11:35 a.m.	la clase de computadoras
1:50 p.m.	el cine	1:15 p.m.	la clase de arte
8:45 p.m.	la casa de la Sra. Millán	7:05 p.m.	el cine

C Make your own schedule for tomorrow's activities. Use these places and activities. Then, ask a partner questions about his or her schedule. See if any of your times match.

> **MODELO** —¿A qué hora vas al cine? *or* ¿Cuándo vas al cine?
>
> —Voy al cine a las cuatro y media de la tarde.

la clase de música	la casa	la tienda
la clase de computadoras	el cine	la escuela
la biblioteca	el gimnasio	el parque
la clase de arte		

CONEXIÓN CON LOS ESTUDIOS SOCIALES

Spanish Explorations Look at the following timeline of some famous explorers from Spain:

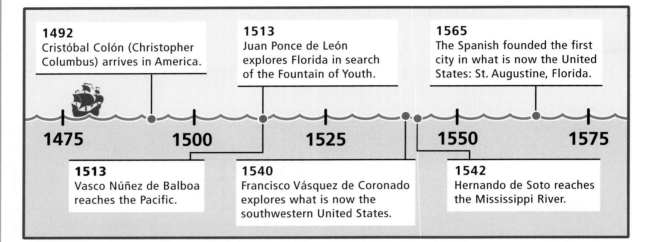

1492
Cristóbal Colón (Christopher Columbus) arrives in America.

1513
Juan Ponce de León explores Florida in search of the Fountain of Youth.

1565
The Spanish founded the first city in what is now the United States: St. Augustine, Florida.

1475   **1500**   **1525**   **1550**   **1575**

1513
Vasco Núñez de Balboa reaches the Pacific.

1540
Francisco Vásquez de Coronado explores what is now the southwestern United States.

1542
Hernando de Soto reaches the Mississippi River.

Now, create your own timeline for a typical day. Draw a line and divide it into 24 hours. Then write or draw the activities that you do at different times. Label your timeline with the following: **la mañana, la tarde, la noche, el mediodía,** and **la medianoche.**

After you finish your timeline, get together with a partner and tell him or her about some of your activities and when you do them.

En resumen

¿Qué hora **es?**	
Es la una.	1:00
Son las tres.	3:00
las tres y cuarto.	3:15
las tres y veinte.	3:20
las tres y media.	3:30
las tres menos veinticinco.	2:35
las tres menos cuarto.	2:45
las tres menos diez.	2:50

Es la una	**en punto.**	1:00
Son las seis	**de la mañana.**	6:00 a. m.
	de la tarde.	6:00 p. m.
Son las nueve	**de la noche.**	9:00 p. m.

¿A qué hora vas a la escuela?
Voy a las ocho menos veinte de la mañana.

¿Cómo se dice?

Asking for information

Some questions only ask for yes-no answers:

¿Vas al cine? ¿Estudias mucho? ¿Tienes suerte?

Other types of questions ask for more information, such as a time of day, a color, or a place. To ask these kinds of questions, you need question words. Different question words ask for different information. You've already been practicing these kinds of questions throughout *¡Hola!*:

> **¿Qué** es?
> **¿Cómo** te llamas?
> **¿Quién** es el chico?
> **¿Cuándo** vas a estudiar?
> **¿Cuál** es tu número de teléfono?
> **¿A qué** hora va a nadar Jorge?
> **¿Cuántos** bolígrafos tienes?
> **¿De qué** color es tu perro?
> **¿Cuánto** tiempo vas a usar la computadora?
> **¿Adónde** vas?
> **¿Qué** hora es?

Notice that the question words come at the beginning of the question. Where does the word indicating the person or thing being referred to—**Jorge, perro**—come in the question?

Compara

En inglés	En español
Who?	¿Quién?
What?	¿Qué?
Where?	¿Dónde?
When?	¿Cuándo?
Why?	¿Por qué?
How?	¿Cómo?
How many?	¿Cuánto(s)? *or* ¿Cuánta(s)?
Which?	¿Cuál?

¡Úsalo!

A Play **"¿Cuál es la pregunta?"** *("What's the Question?")* with a partner. Read the answer and question choices aloud. Point to the correct picture for the answer. Your partner must choose the right question. Switch roles after each item.

> **MODELO** **El ratón es pequeño.**
> **a.** ¿Cómo se llama el ratón?
> **b.** ¿De qué color es el ratón?
> **c.** **¿Cómo es el ratón?**

1. Voy a la escuela.
   a. ¿Cuándo vas tú?
   b. ¿Adónde vas?
   c. ¿A qué hora vas?

2. Me llamo Esteban Llosa.
   a. ¿Quién es el chico?
   b. ¿Qué son?
   c. ¿Cómo te llamas?

3. Son las tres menos cuarto.
   a. ¿Qué día es hoy?
   b. ¿A qué hora estudias?
   c. ¿Qué hora es?

4. Tengo veinte loros.
   a. ¿Cuántos loros tienes?
   b. ¿Qué son?
   c. ¿Cómo son los loros?

5. Estudio a las diez.
   a. ¿Qué hora es?
   b. ¿Adónde vas?
   c. ¿A qué hora estudia usted?

6. Son unos bolígrafos.
   a. ¿Cuántos bolígrafos tienes?
   b. ¿Qué son?
   c. ¿Quiénes son?

B You and a friend are with a visitor from Uruguay. The visitor keeps asking you questions, but the school band is practicing next door, and you can only hear part of the questions. Your visitor has to repeat the entire question.

Partner A: Complete and ask the entire question.

Partner B: Answer the question truthfully.

> **MODELO** ¿ _____ hora vas a la escuela?
> —¿A qué hora vas a la escuela?
> —Voy a la escuela a las ocho y media.

1. ¿_____ te llamas?
2. ¿_____ años tienes?
3. ¿_____ es tu profesor?
4. ¿_____ hora estudias en casa?
5. ¿_____ alumnos hay en tu clase de arte?
6. ¿_____ estación te gusta?
7. ¿_____ tiempo hace en verano?
8. ¿_____ vas esta semana?
9. ¿_____ color es tu perro?
10. ¿_____ vas al parque?

¿Qué es el tiempo?
El tiempo es oro.

C Get together with a partner. Fill out questionnaires like this one about each other. Take turns asking one another questions so that you can fill it out.

MODELO **Hora de ir a la escuela:** _____

—¿A qué hora vas a la escuela?

—Voy a la escuela a las ocho y media.

Nombre: _____

Edad (Age): _____

Tu maestro favorito: _____

**El número de alumnos
en el salón de clase:** _____

Tu animal favorito: _____

Hora de ir a la escuela: _____

Hora de ir a estudiar: _____

Hora de ir a jugar: _____

Tu clase favorita: _____

**Tu actividad los
fines de semana:** _____

¿Sabías que...?

You already know that English has "borrowed" many words, such as **mesa,** from Spanish. But did you know that some words in English also find their way into Spanish? The word *stress,* for example, has become **estrés** in Spanish! Although it's spelled differently, it sounds almost the same and means the same thing in both languages.

CONEXIÓN CON LA SALUD

Stress Stress is a condition that not only affects grown-ups—it can also affect you. Stress can cause problems by itself, or it can make you worse when you get sick. To find out whether you're stressed, get together with a partner and ask each other these questions.

1. ¿Tienes sueño por la mañana?
2. ¿Tienes sueño por la noche?
3. ¿Estás bien por la mañana?
4. ¿Te gusta caminar? ¿Caminas mucho?
5. ¿Te gusta nadar?
6. ¿Te gusta dibujar?
7. ¿Te gusta practicar deportes?
8. ¿Tienes prisa los días de la semana?
9. ¿Tienes prisa los fines de semana?

Score one point for each **Sí** answer to questions 2 through 7; zero points for each **No.**

Score zero points for **Sí** answers to questions 1, 8, and 9; one point for each **No.**

How many points did you get? How many points did your partner get?

If you get zero points, start thinking of some ways to manage your stress better.

◎ ◎ ◎ Compara ◎ ◎ ◎

En inglés	En español
stress	el estrés

En resumen

¿**Qué** es?
¿**Cómo** te llamas?
¿**Quién** es el chico?
¿**Cuándo** vas a estudiar?
¿**Cuál** es tu número de teléfono?
¿**A qué** hora va a nadar Jorge?

¿**Cuántos** bolígrafos tienes tú?
¿**De qué** color es tu perro?
¿**Cuánto** tiempo vas a usar la computadora?
¿**Adónde** vas?
¿**Qué** hora es?

¿Dónde se habla español?

Buenos Aires

Argentina

Argentina is a large country that extends to the tip of South America. Its southernmost point is called **Tierra del Fuego,** which means "Land of Fire." The explorer Magellan gave the land this name in 1520 because of the many bonfires he saw at night from his ship. Since then, many people have settled in

◎◎◎◎◎ Datos ◎◎◎◎◎◎

Capital: Buenos Aires

Ciudades importantes: Córdoba, Mendoza, Rosario, Tucumán, La Plata

Idioma oficial: Español

Moneda: El peso argentino

Población: 38.7 millones

Argentina. Did you know that the tallest mountain peak in the Western Hemisphere is in the Argentine Andes? It's Mount Aconcagua, and it's 22,831 feet tall (6,960 m)! In the region where Argentina, Paraguay, and Brazil meet, you can see the spectacular Iguazú Falls (pictured on the next page). They're only about 237 feet tall, but they're almost two miles wide! The area around the falls is a national park. If you go to the southern region of Patagonia, you'll see glacial lakes and meet some of the indigenous people who still live in Argentina.

The people of Buenos Aires are called **porteños** and enjoy the many advantages of this cosmopolitan city: wide boulevards, outdoor cafés, elegant stores, world-class restaurants, museums, parks, and theaters. **Los porteños** also enjoy watching or dancing **el tango,** a dramatic dance originated in Buenos Aires.

Reading Strategy

Recognizing Cognates What do you think these words mean: **centro, región, agricultura, exportación, rancho?** Use these cognates to help you understand what is being said about Argentina.

¡Léelo en español!

El gaucho y las pampas Las pampas son unas grandes llanuras[1] en el centro de Argentina. Es una región importante para la agricultura y el ganado[2]. Mucha de la comida[3] para los argentinos y para la exportación es de esta región. En las pampas también trabajan los gauchos. Los gauchos son los *cowboys* argentinos. Cuidan[4] muy bien el ganado. Los gauchos trabajan mucho: desde[5] la salida del sol hasta[6] la puesta del sol. Por la noche los gauchos van a las estancias, que son unos ranchos especiales.

¡Comprendo!

Complete these statements about **"El gaucho y las pampas"** on a separate sheet of paper.

1. **Las pampas** are . . .
2. **Las pampas** are important because . . .
3. **El gaucho** is a . . .
4. **El gaucho's** job is . . .
5. **Los gauchos** work . . .

[1] plains   [2] cattle   [3] food   [4] They take care of
[5] from   [6] to

Mis clases favoritas...

Objetivos

- To talk about classes you like (and classes you don't like!)
- To give your opinion about different things
- To talk about your likes and dislikes
- To talk about things you do in school and make schedules

Cerro Tololo observatory in Chile

Kids in San Vicente, El Salvador, play basketball.

A weekly class schedule made by a Spanish student

HORARIO DE ACTIVIDADES ESCOLARES

HORAS	LUNES	MARTES	MIÉRCOLES	JUEVES	VIERNES
9-10	MATE	INGLÈS	RELIGION	INGLÈS	MATE
10-10.45	VALENCIANO	MATE	VALENCIANO	MATE	MATE
10.45-11.15	R E C R E O				
11.15-12.15	CASTELLANO	CASTELLANO	CASTELLANO	INGLÈS	RELIGION
12.15-13	E.F	CONOCIMIENTO DEL MEDIO	CONOCIMIENTO DEL MEDIO	VALENCIANO	E.F
15-15.45	MÙSICA	PLÀSTICA		CONOCIMIENTO DEL MEDIO	CONOCIMIENTO DEL MEDIO
15.45-16.30	RELIGION	PLÀSTICA		CONOCIMIENTO DEL MEDIO	MÙSICA

¿Sabías que...?

In Spanish-speaking countries:

- The most popular foreign language course is English.

- Many activities like sports, art, and music often aren't sponsored by schools. Kids do them at local clubs.

- Kids in fourth grade study about nine or ten different subjects each week!

¿Cómo se dice?

What's your favorite class?

—¿Cuál es tu clase favorita?

—¡El español, claro!

el español

las ciencias

la salud

el inglés

la lectura

las matemáticas

los estudios sociales

la educación física

¿Sabías que...?

In many Spanish-speaking countries, students get graded on a point system from 1 to 10. Ten is the best grade a student can get. To pass an exam you usually need to get at least 5 points. If you get 9 to 10 points, it's called **un sobresaliente.** This means "outstanding"!

¡Úsalo!

A Get together with three or four classmates. On different cards, draw things that you use or learn in each class. Exchange your cards with a different group. Take turns picking out cards and guessing the class!

> **MODELO** —¿Qué clase es?
>
> —¡Es la clase de matemáticas!

B Think of the perfect school schedule for yourself. Write three classes for each day on a schedule like this one. You can choose how many times a week you will take each class. Get together with a partner and ask each other when each class takes place.

lunes	martes	miércoles	jueves	viernes

> **MODELO** —¿Cuándo es la clase de música?
>
> —¡El lunes, el martes, el miércoles y el jueves!

 **Entre amigos**

Write the names of each class you know on different cards. Get together with a partner and mix your cards together. Place them facedown in rows on a table or desk. Turn over two cards to see if they match. If they match, keep the cards and take another turn. If they don't match, your partner takes a turn.

CONEXIÓN CON LAS MATEMÁTICAS

Fractions Ask three people in your class this question:

¿Cuál es tu clase favorita?

Keep track of their answers.

Now work with the rest of your class. Pick one of your classmates to go to the board and make a chart that looks like this one:

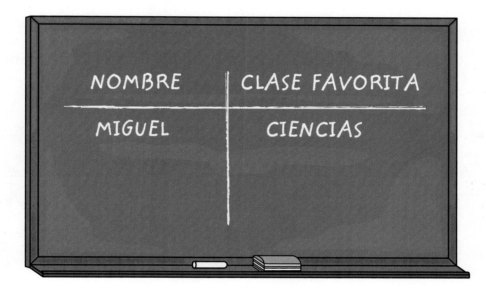

NOMBRE	CLASE FAVORITA
MIGUEL	CIENCIAS

One student calls out the name of a person in class. If you hear the name of someone you interviewed, say that person's favorite class. The person at the chalkboard adds the information to the chart.

When everybody's name has been called, add up the answers. What are the five most popular classes? Figure out the fraction of the class that prefers each one. Write the classes in order from most popular to least and include the fractions.

En resumen

el español
el inglés
los estudios sociales

la educación física
la lectura
la salud
las ciencias
las matemáticas

¿Cómo se dice?

What's your opinion?

—¿Te gusta la clase de ciencias?

—Sí, me gusta mucho.

—¿Por qué?

—¡Es fantástica!

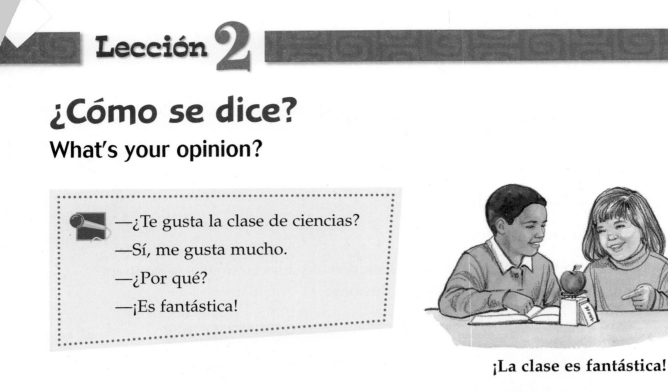

¡La clase es fantástica!

—¿Te gusta la clase de salud?

—¡Ay, no!

—¿Por qué no?

—¡Es aburrida!

¡La clase es aburrida!

¡La clase es divertida!   **¡Es fácil!**   **¡Es difícil!**

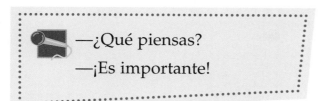

—¿Qué piensas?

—¡Es importante!

¡Es importante!

¡Es interesante!

¡Es terrible!

CONEXIÓN CON LA SALUD

Active Lifestyles Physical education classes are not only fun—they also promote healthful habits! In many Spanish-speaking countries, as in most other parts of the world, people don't use their cars as much as people in the United States do. People walk more or take public transportation. In the United States, people who live in cities are usually fitter than people who live in the suburbs. That's because they don't have to drive everywhere! How much do *you* walk on a typical day? Say in Spanish the time you spend walking.

¿Sabías que...?

When Spanish-speaking students really like something, they may also say:

¡Es sensacional!   ¡Es espectacular!

¡Es fabuloso(a)!   ¡Es magnífico(a)!

¡Es maravilloso(a)!   ¡Es fantástico(a)!

¡Úsalo!

A Get together with a partner. Ask each other if you like these things, and why. Do you like the same things?

Partner A: Ask whether your partner likes the things on the list, and why.

Partner B: Answer with the expressions in the column on the right.

MODELO   —¿Te gusta el español?

—Sí, claro.

—¿Por qué?

—Porque es interesante.

1. estudiar español	
2. ir al cine	es fantástico(a)
3. practicar deportes	es aburrido(a)
4. usar la computadora	es fácil
5. el verano	es difícil
6. limpiar el salón de clase	es importante
7. caminar en el parque	es interesante
8. dibujar	es terrible
9. la clase de matemáticas	es divertido(a)
10. estudiar los fines de semana	

B Get together with a partner. Ask each other what you think of each painting or sculpture.

MODELO —¿Qué piensas?

—¡Es fantástico!

1.

2.

3.

4.

CONEXIÓN CON EL ARTE

Now, be a real art critic! With a partner, look through art books and talk about what you think of each painting. Find at least one painting for each of the expressions that you have learned.

En resumen

¿Qué piensas?	(el cine) ¡Es	fantástico!	(la escuela) ¡Es	fácil!
(la clase) ¡Es fantástica!		aburrido!	(el libro)	terrible!
aburrida!		divertido!		difícil!
divertida!				importante!
				interesante!

Lección 3

¿Cómo se dice?

Talking about things you like

You already know how to talk about something you like:

Me gusta el libro.   **¿Te gusta** el pez?   A Inés **le gusta** el loro.

But what happens when there's more than one thing? Look at these examples:

Me gustan los libros.   **¿Te gustan** los peces?   A Inés **le gustan** los loros.

Did you notice that you say **gustan** instead of **gusta** when you're talking about more than one thing?

¡Úsalo!

A Make a chart like this one and answer the survey about your likes and dislikes. Put a check mark in the appropriate boxes.

Then get together with three or four classmates. Exchange surveys with the person on your right and tell everyone in the group what he or she likes and dislikes.

	Me gusta	Me gustan	No me gusta	No me gustan
los deportes				✔
las bibliotecas				
los libros de matemáticas				
la pizza				
las computadoras				
el frío				
los perros				
bailar				
la música				
los mapas				
cantar	✔			
la escuela				

MODELO —A Sara no le gustan los deportes. Le gusta cantar.

¿Sabías que...?

Another way for Spanish speakers to say that they really love something is ¡Me encanta! or ¡Me encantan!

B Play an acting game! Get together with three or four classmates and play against another team. Each team writes sentences about what they like on five different cards.

One person from Team A picks a card from Team B and acts out the sentence. Team A has to guess what the team member is acting out before a minute goes by! Each correct answer earns a point. Then it's Team B's turn to pick a card and guess.

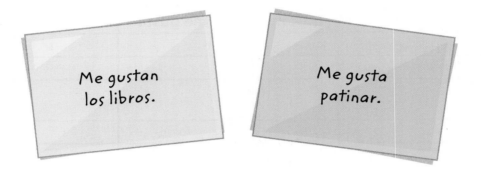

Me gustan los libros.

Me gusta patinar.

CONEXIÓN CON EL ARTE

Look for examples of paintings and sculptures in magazines. Choose two you like and two you don't like, and then cut them out. Get together with a partner and explain why you like and why you dislike your choices. Tape up the ones that you like in the classroom.

◎ ◎ ◎ Compara ◎ ◎ ◎

En inglés	En español
sculpture	la escultura
painting	la pintura

C Get together with a partner. Find the differences in these pictures of Claudia! Cover one of the pictures with a sheet of paper, while your partner covers the other one. Ask each other about the things Claudia likes. Answer each other according to your own picture.

Partner A: Ask questions about Claudia, according to your picture.

Partner B: Answer the questions according to your picture.

MODELO —¿A Claudia le gusta la música?
—Umm... sí.

En inglés	En español
tennis	el tenis
basketball	el básquetbol

Entre amigos

Here's your chance to find out what your friends like and don't like.

Take a sheet of paper. You need to make a list of six items to ask about. Look at the six categories shown to the right. Think of an item that fits each one. Write the items on your paper.

Ask a partner if he or she likes the things on your list:

—¿Te gusta (el español)?
—¡Sí, me gusta mucho! *or* No, no me gusta.

Write down the answers. When the teacher calls your partner's name, tell the class what you've learned about him or her.

—A Tomás no le gusta (el español). Le gusta mucho (la educación física).

Categories:
1. A school subject you like
2. A school subject you don't like
3. An animal you like
4. An animal you don't like
5. A day of the week
6. A season of the year

En resumen

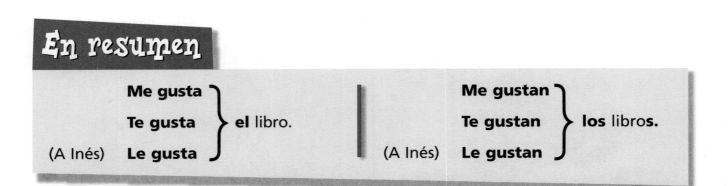

	Me gusta				Me gustan	
	Te gusta	} el libro.			Te gustan	} los libros.
(A Inés)	Le gusta			(A Inés)	Le gustan	

¿Cómo se dice?

What do you do in school?

What's the main reason you come to school? To learn things!
The verb that means "to learn" is **aprender.** Here's how you use it:

Aprendo español.

¿Aprendes español?

¿Aprende usted español?

Él **aprende** español.

Ella **aprende** español.

Did you notice the different endings on the verb?

Aprendo a pintar.

Did you notice the word **a** before the word that says what you are learning to do? You always need it after the verb **aprender** if you're talking about an activity that you're learning to do.

The verb **escribir** means "to write." Here's how you use it:

Escribo en el pizarrón.

Tú **escribes** en el pizarrón también.

Usted **escribe** en el pizarrón.

Él **escribe** en el pizarrón.

Ella **escribe** en el pizarrón.

Most verbs that end in **–er** and **–ir** use these same endings, so if you know the endings for one verb, you know the endings for all the verbs in that group.

For example, the verb **leer** means "to read." How would you tell someone that you're reading a book? How would you ask a friend if she's reading?

Another important verb to know when you're learning Spanish is **comprender,** which means "to understand."

—¿**Comprendes?**

—**No, no comprendo.** *or* ¡**Sí, comprendo!**

¡Úsalo!

A Choose five things from the list below and write them on different cards. Get together with a partner and mix your cards together. Each person gets five. Ask your partner what he or she learns in school. Your partner answers according to the cards he or she has. Write down the answers.

Partner A: Ask your partner if he or she learns the items on the list.

Partner B: Answer according to the cards you have.

> **MODELO** —¿Aprendes a hablar español?
>
> —Sí, aprendo a hablar español.

1. matemáticas
2. cantar
3. pintar
4. ciencias
5. patinar
6. usar la computadora
7. estudios sociales
8. lectura
9. español
10. leer

When you finish, switch partners. Tell each other what your first partner said. Did both partners learn the same things?

¿Sabías que...?

Did you remember that the Spanish alphabet has more letters than the English alphabet? The Spanish alphabet includes the letters **ch, ll,** and **ñ.** You've seen these letters in words like **noche, llamo,** and **español.** What other words do you know that include these letters?

B Play a game of quick **"sí"** questions. Make up a question for each item on the list below. Think about who is likely to answer with **"sí"** and ask that classmate the question.

If your classmate answers **"sí,"** you get to ask someone the next question. If they say no, you have to keep asking other classmates the same question until you get a **"sí."**

Don't forget to ask your teacher too, if you think he or she will say **"sí"**!

MODELO	—¿Lees muchos libros?

—**Sí, leo muchos libros.** *or* **No, no leo muchos libros.**

1. aprender a pintar
2. practicar deportes en el verano
3. usar la computadora por la noche
4. comprender las matemáticas
5. caminar a la escuela
6. limpiar la casa los sábados

After you finish asking your questions, write sentences about the people who said **"sí."**

MODELO	Laura lee muchos libros.

C Help create a class biography book! Your teacher will assign you a partner. Using the kinds of questions you practiced in this lesson, interview your partner. After you have both asked and answered the questions, write a six-sentence paragraph about your partner. Your teacher will combine the biographies you write to make a class biography book!

CONEXIÓN CON LAS MATEMÁTICAS

Making a Schedule Make a chart with the days of the week across the top and the times for classes down the side. Then fill in a week's schedule in Spanish for your partner with information you make up.

You can even have classes on Saturdays! Some classes could start very early in the morning and others very late at night. Some classes may last for hours, while others may last only minutes!

	lunes	martes	miércoles	jueves	viernes	sábado	domingo
6:00 a. m.							
7:00 a. m.							
8:00 a. m.							

When you're done, read the schedule to your partner and see how he or she reacts.

MODELO —El lunes tienes clase de matemáticas a las seis de la mañana.

—¡Ay, no! ¡Es terrible!

En resumen

	aprender	**escribir**	**leer**	**comprender**	**endings**
	aprend-	escrib-	le-	comprend-	
yo	aprend**o**	escrib**o**	le**o**	comprend**o**	**-o**
tú	aprend**es**	escrib**es**	le**es**	comprend**es**	**-es**
él					
ella	aprend**e**	escrib**e**	le**e**	comprend**e**	**-e**
usted					

¿Dónde se habla español?

Chicago

Nueva York

ESTADOS UNIDOS (U.S.)

PUERTO RICO

Puerto Ricans in the United States

As you already know, Puerto Rico is an island in the Caribbean. After the Spanish-American War of 1898, in which Spain lost all rights to the island, Puerto Rico became a commonwealth of the United States, or **un estado libre asociado.** Because Puerto Ricans are U.S. citizens, they can travel without restrictions between the island and the mainland. Many **puertorriqueños** have chosen to emigrate and settle around major cities on the mainland, since there are often better job opportunities. About 3.1 million people of Puerto Rican descent are now living on the mainland United States. Almost 800,000 live in New York City alone,

making it the second largest Puerto Rican population after San Juan! Chicago's Puerto Rican population is of approximately 100,000.

Puerto Rican parade in Bronx, New York

¡Léelo en español!

Dos puertorriqueños famosos en los Estados Unidos

Soy Ricky Martin. Soy de Puerto Rico pero ahora vivo en los Estados Unidos. Canto y bailo en la televisión y en los conciertos. También canto y bailo en la presentación de los Grammy. Gano[1] muchos premios.[2] ¡Tengo mucho talento! Soy joven, guapo y muy simpático. Soy actor también en la televisión y en las telenovelas.[3] Con mi dinero y mi fama, me gusta ayudar[4] a los niños del mundo.

[1] I win   [2] awards   [3] soap operas   [4] help

Me llamo Roberto Clemente.[1] Soy de Puerto Rico. Soy un hombre muy dedicado al deporte. Soy jugador de béisbol. Es mi pasión. El béisbol es muy popular en los Estados Unidos y en Puerto Rico. Juego con los Piratas de Pittsburg. Me gusta ayudar a las personas de Puerto Rico y de otros países[2] del mundo. Es importante ayudar a las personas. Soy el primer hispano que está en el *"Baseball Hall of Fame"* en Cooperstown, Nueva York. Y soy el segundo jugador de béisbol que tiene su foto en un sello.[3]

[1] Clemente lived from 1934 to 1972. He was killed in an airplane accident on New Year's Eve while on his way to help victims of an earthquake in Nicaragua.   [2] other countries   [3] stamp

Reading Strategy

Using What You Know

Before you start to read, look at the pictures of the two people. Do you recognize them? Read their names. Have you ever heard of them? If so, you might guess what the reading is about. Using what you know helps you be a better reader.

Recognizing Cognates
What do you think these words mean: **conciertos, presentación, talento, dedicado, pasión?** Use these cognates to help you understand what is being said about these famous Puerto Ricans.

¡Comprendo!

Answer in English.

1. What is Ricky Martin known for? Did you learn anything about him you didn't know before?

2. What is Roberto Clemente known for? Did you learn anything about him you didn't know before?

3. Who are some other famous Puerto Ricans who have come to live in the United States?

Mi familia y yo

Objetivos

- To talk about family members
- To talk about who owns things
- To describe people

A family strolls through Alameda del Tajo Park in Ronda, Spain.

A large family gathers in the Andes

A Spanish bride and her father walk past guests in Madrid.

¿Sabías que...?

In Spanish-speaking countries:

- People often spend Sunday afternoons with grandparents, aunts, uncles, and cousins.

- Brothers, sisters, and cousins see one another often, going shopping, to parties, to the movies, and other places together.

- It's common for grandparents, especially if they are widowed, to live with their children and grandchildren.

Lección 1

¿Cómo se dice?

What are their names?

—¿Cómo se llama la mamá de Alicia?

—Se llama Beatriz Muñoz.

Javier Muñoz   Beatriz Muñoz

mi papá   mi mamá
mi padre   mi madre

Mis padres

Los Muñoz

Felipe · Adriana · Rosa · Alicia

mi hermano · mi hermana · mi hermanita · yo

Here are some additional words that describe other family members:

el padrastro—*stepfather*
la madrastra—*stepmother*
el hermanastro—*stepbrother*
la hermanastra—*stepsister*

Mis hermanos y yo

¿Sabías que...?

Did you notice that Alicia uses the word **hermanita?** That's because Spanish speakers use the endings **-ito** or **-ita** to say that someone or something is small or younger. You can also use these endings to show that a person or thing is special to you.

¡Úsalo!

A This is Linda's family. Get together with a partner and ask each other these questions about her family.

Juan Guajardo

Susana Guajardo

Alberto

David

Linda

Marisa

1. ¿Cómo se llama la mamá de Linda?
2. ¿Cómo se llama el papá de Linda?
3. ¿Cuántas hermanas tiene Linda?
4. ¿Cómo se llama su hermana?
5. ¿Cuántos hermanos tiene Linda?
6. ¿Cómo se llama la hermanita de David?

B Ask a partner questions about the members of his or her family. Ask for their names and ages. Use the answers to draw your partner's family tree. You can talk about your real family or a make-believe family.

¿Sabías que...?

When Spanish speakers talk about several people who are a mix of boys and girls or men and women, they always use **los**:

la **hermana** + *el* **hermano** = *los hermanos*
el **padre** + *la* **madre** = *los padres*
el **maestro** + *la* **maestra** = *los maestros*

CONEXIÓN CON LAS MATEMÁTICAS

Making a Bar Graph Get together with three or four classmates. Take a class survey to see how many students have a certain number of brothers and sisters. Divide up the names of the people in your class so that each of you only has to ask a third or a quarter of your classmates. (Be sure to include yourselves.) Make a list like this one to keep track of the answers. Write a check mark for each person who responds.

0	hermanos	_____
1	hermano	_____
2	hermanos	_____
3	hermanos	_____
4	hermanos	_____
5+	hermanos	_____

Once your group has the information, make a bar graph like this one to show the results:

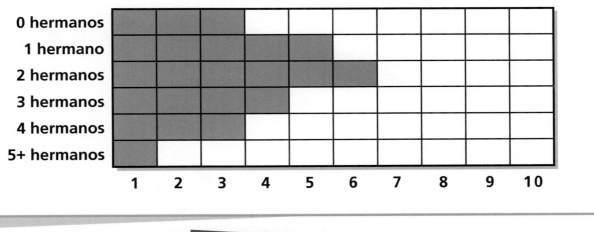

En resumen

el papá		la mamá
el padre		la madre
el padrastro	**de** Alicia	la madrastra
el hermano		la hermana
el hermanastro		la hermanastra

¿Cómo se dice?

Who is who?

—¿Quién es el hijo de Sandra?

—Miguelito es el hijo de Sandra.

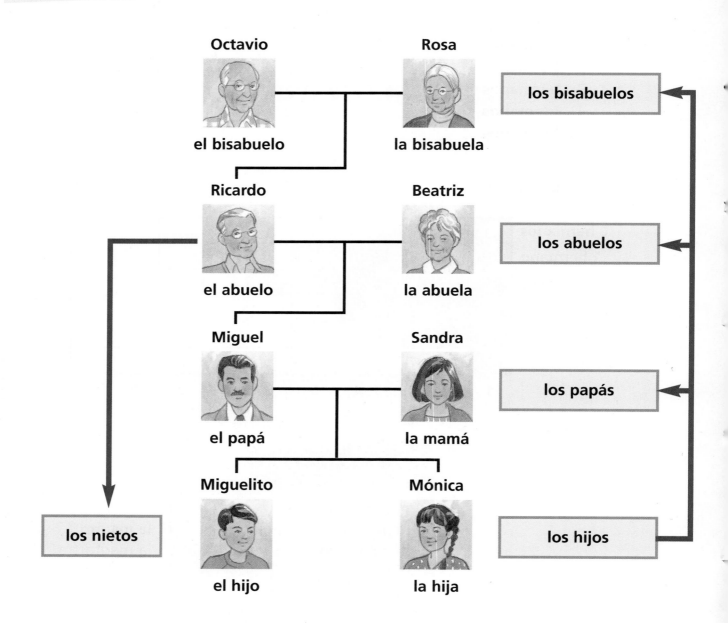

Octavio — el bisabuelo

Rosa — la bisabuela

los bisabuelos

Ricardo — el abuelo

Beatriz — la abuela

los abuelos

Miguel — el papá

Sandra — la mamá

los papás

los nietos

Miguelito — el hijo

Mónica — la hija

los hijos

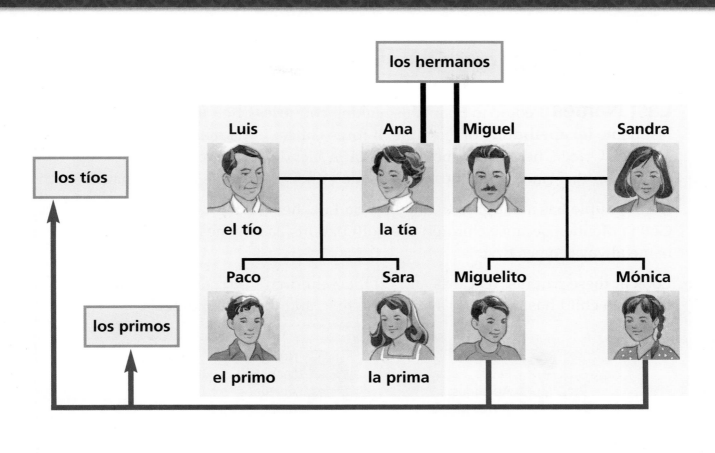

los hermanos

Luis — el tío

Ana — la tía

Miguel

Sandra

Paco — el primo

Sara — la prima

Miguelito

Mónica

los tíos

los primos

—¿Quién es la tía de Mónica?

—Ana es su tía.

¿Sabías que...?

Spanish speakers show respect by addressing older people or those in positions of authority as **don** or **doña**—**don** for men and **doña** for women. These titles are used with the person's first name, not the family name: **don José, doña Amalia.**

CONEXIÓN CON LA CULTURA

Last Names People in Spanish-speaking countries often use more than one last name **(el apellido).** For example, if Jorge García Luna marries Ana María Méndez Ortega, her new name is Ana María Méndez de García. Women keep the first of their maiden names and add **de +** their husband's first last name.

If this couple has a daughter named María Luz, her full name is María Luz García Méndez because children use both parents' last names. The father's last name always comes first.

Look at these parents' ID cards and fill their children's out correctly. Remember that each child has the father's last name first, and then the mother's.

Nombre:
Pedro
Apellidos:
Torres Martín

Nombre:
Leonela
Apellidos:
Ginés Sánchez

Nombre:
Javier
Apellidos:

Nombre:
Adriana
Apellidos:

Compare the last names you wrote with those your partner wrote.

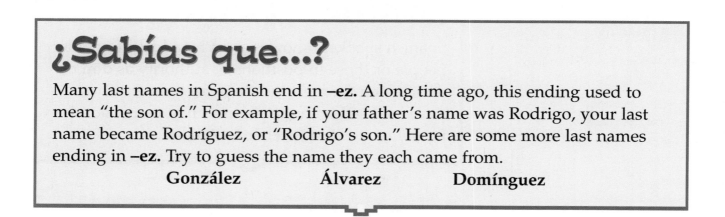

¿Sabías que...?

Many last names in Spanish end in **–ez.** A long time ago, this ending used to mean "the son of." For example, if your father's name was Rodrigo, your last name became Rodríguez, or "Rodrigo's son." Here are some more last names ending in **–ez.** Try to guess the name they each came from.

González   **Álvarez**   **Domínguez**

¡Úsalo!

Look at this family tree with a partner. Tell each other about the relationships between the different members of the family.

MODELO Don Eduardo es el bisabuelo de Carlos. Carlos es el nieto de doña Anita.

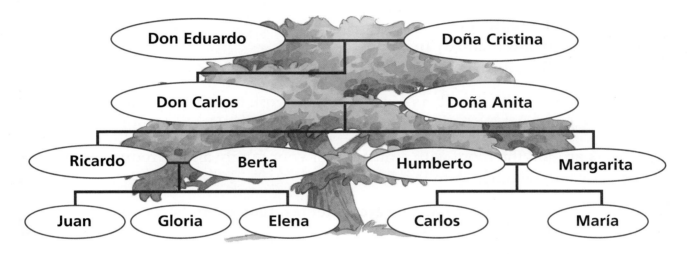

CONEXIÓN CON LOS ESTUDIOS SOCIALES

Family Trees Create an extended family tree! Get together with two classmates. Your teacher will give you some cards about the members of a family. Look at the people, their ages, and their last names. Write their names on a poster. Draw lines to show the relationships between different people. Introduce the family to the rest of the class.

MODELO Se llama Fernando. Es el bisabuelo de Andrea.

Ella se llama Carmen y es la abuela de Andrea…

Entre amigos

You're going to form a "family" with other classmates, but first you need to find all the family members! Your teacher will give each of you a card with the name and picture of a person. You're going to play this person.

Ask your classmates for their full names to find your "relatives." There will be several families in the room!

> —¿Cómo te llamas?
> —Me llamo Juan Álvarez Fuentes. ¿Y tú?
> —Me llamo Adriana Álvarez Fuentes.

Once you find the members of your family, work together to figure out all the relationships between the different members. Draw a family tree.

Walk around the room with a member of your family and introduce your relative to the other "families."

> —Me llamo Adriana Álvarez Fuentes. Juan es mi hermano. Tiene quince años.

En resumen

¿Quién es la abuela de Elena?
Doña Carmen es la abuela de Elena.

¿Quién es Elena?
Es la nieta de doña Carmen.

el abuelo	la abuela	los abuelos
el bisabuelo	la bisabuela	los bisabuelos
el hijo	la hija	los hijos
el nieto	la nieta	los nietos
el primo	la prima	los primos
el tío	la tía	los tíos

¿Cómo se dice?

Talking about whom things belong to

Study these pictures and sentences. What word do you use to say that something belongs to you? What word do you use to say that something belongs to someone else?

¡Es **mi** perro!   ¿Es **tu** perro?   Señor, ¿es **su** perro?

Es **su** perro.   Es **su** perro.

Use **mi** to talk about something that belongs to you. When you're talking to a friend about something that belongs to him or her, use **tu.** When you're talking to an adult, use **su.** Finally, when you want to talk about something that belongs to someone else —either a boy or a girl, a man or a woman—use **su** as well.

How do you think these words change when you're talking about more than one of something? Look at these sentences.

Es **mi** primo.

Son **mis** primos.

Es **tu** abuelo.

Son **tus** abuelos.

¿Es **su** hija?

¿Son **sus** hijas?

All you have to do is add an **-s** to the word that shows possession. **Mi** becomes **mis, tu** becomes **tus,** and **su** becomes **sus.**

You can also show possession by using the word **de** plus the name of the person who owns the item. It's like using *'s* in English.

El libro es **de** Sonia. *(It's Sonia's book.)*
La regla es **de** la maestra. *(It's the teacher's ruler.)*

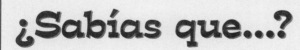

¿Sabías que...?

When you write, be sure not to confuse **tú** with **tu.** The accent mark makes the difference between saying "you" and "your." With the accent, it's "you"; without, it's "your."

¡Úsalo!

A Draw an object you know in Spanish on a card, and on another card, draw several of the same object. Write your name on both cards. Get together with three classmates. Put all the cards in a box and take turns drawing cards and saying who they belong to. Talk to the person on your right and say if the object is yours, his or hers, or if it belongs to someone else in the group.

> **MODELO** —**Son tus bolígrafos.**

B Draw a picture of your family or of a make-believe family. Get together with a partner and introduce everyone in your family.

> **MODELO** —**Es mi mamá. Se llama Rosa. Tiene 35 años.**

Now your partner tells you who everyone is, just to make sure he or she got it right.

> **MODELO** —**Es tu mamá. Es tu hermana.**

After your partner has talked about his or her family, exchange drawings and switch partners. Show your new partner the drawing and talk about your first partner's family.

> **MODELO** —**Es la familia de Rebeca. Son sus papás. Su mamá se llama...**

Entre amigos

Get together with a group of six people. Use someone's empty backpack, or a large bag. Each person in the group should put in at least two different school items, such as **un libro, un lápiz, una regla,** or **un cuaderno.** Make sure your name is on each item that belongs to you.

Get in a circle with your group. One person starts by reaching into the bag, pulling out an item, and asking **¿Qué es?**

The person to his or her left takes the item(s), looks at the name, and answers:

> **Es mi regla.** *or* **Son tus bolígrafos.** *or* **Es su libro.** (pointing to the appropriate person)

Put the item aside, pass the bag to the left, and continue the game. The person responding must do so quickly. See if your group can finish before the other groups.

En resumen

Es **mi** primo.
Es **tu** abuelo.
Es **su** papá.

Son **mis** primos.
Son **tus** abuelos.
Son **sus** papás.

¿Cómo se dice?

Describing people

You already know how to describe the color and size of an animal or an object. Now look at these descriptions of people.

El papá es **alto.**

Los papás son **altos.**

Mi hermana es **baja.**

Mis hermanas son **bajas.**

Mi primo es **simpático.**

Mis primos son **simpáticos.**

Mi prima es **antipática.**

Mis primas son **antipáticas.**

Susana es **joven.**

El señor Medina es **viejo.**

Roberto es **guapo.**

Notice how most of these descriptive words change when we talk about females and males, and when we talk about more than one. As with other descriptive words, add an **–s** if the descriptive word ends in a vowel and an **–es** if it does not end in a vowel.

Did you notice that the word **joven** does not change whether it describes a male or a female?

Mi hermano es simpátic**o**.   Mi hermana es simpátic**a**.

Mi papá es **joven.**   Mi mamá es **joven.**

But look what happens when more than one person is described as **joven:**

Mis primos son **jóvenes.**
Mis padres son **jóvenes.**

¿Sabías que...?

In Spanish, the word **joven** can also mean "young man" or "young woman." For example, you could say **La joven es alta y simpática.** But watch out if you use **viejo!** Many people don't like to be called *old*. Spanish speakers often use other words to avoid calling someone **viejo** or **vieja**.

CONEXIÓN CON LA SALUD

Family Resemblance Do you look like your dad? Or do you look more like your mom? We inherit some physical and personality traits from our parents. We also sometimes learn to act like the people we live with, even if we're not related by blood.

Find out if your partner resembles members of his or her family. Ask your partner questions about each member of the family. Show your partner's answers on a chart like this one. If you don't have brothers or sisters, use **primos** and **primas** or **tíos** and **tías** instead.

MODELO —¿Cómo es tu mamá?

—Es baja, simpática y guapa.

	alto/a	bajo/a	simpático/a	antipático/a	guapo/a
mamá					
papá					
hermano					
hermana					
abuelo					
abuela					

Then look at your partner and think about his or her characteristics. Find ways in which your partner resembles a member of his or her family. Tell your class about it.

MODELO —Carol es alta. Su mamá también es alta.

¡Úsalo!

A Look at these photos of famous people. Get together with a partner. Choose a photo without telling your partner who it is. Describe the person. Your partner has to guess the person you're describing.

> **MODELO** —Es baja, guapa y muy simpática.
> —Es Penélope Cruz.

Penélope Cruz

Antonio Banderas

Andy García

Gloria Estéfan

Óscar de la Hoya

Enrique Iglesias

Cameron Díaz

B Cut out five pictures of people from magazines. Put them with those of the rest of the class on a bulletin board.

Secretly choose one of the pictures posted. Write a few sentences about the person. Include how old you think the person is, if he or she is tall or short, and whether the person looks friendly or not.

When you finish, read the description to the class. See who can guess the correct picture first!

Entre amigos

Get together with a partner. Draw your partner's family, as if it were a photo. You want to be very accurate, so first you need to know everything you can about his or her family. You can ask:

¿Cuántos hermanos tienes?
¿Cómo es tu mamá?
¿Cómo se llama tu papá?
¿Tienes abuelos?

Now draw your partner's family. Add everyone's names, ages, and relationship to your partner. Show your partner the drawing. Is everything correct? Have your partner fix any mistakes.

CONEXIÓN CON LAS MATEMÁTICAS

Look at these birthdates. Figure out the age of each person and then decide if the person is young or old. Compare your answers with those of a partner.

el 7 de enero de 1954   **el 10 de julio de 1930**
el 24 de mayo de 1986   **el 8 de septiembre de 1990**

En resumen

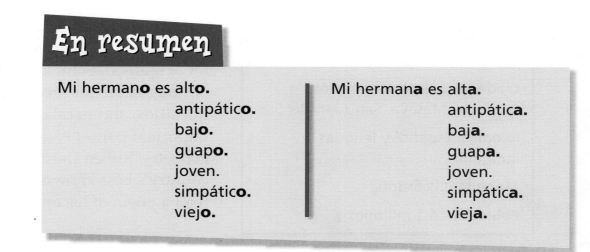

Mi hermano es alto.	Mi hermana es alta.
antipático.	antipática.
bajo.	baja.
guapo.	guapa.
joven.	joven.
simpático.	simpática.
viejo.	vieja.

¿Dónde se habla español?

Nicaragua

Beaches, volcanoes, and nature preserves await you in Nicaragua. You can hike in tropical forests, rain forests and cloud forests. You can swim or snorkel at many of the tiny islands off its shores or in the giant **Lago Nicaragua.** On the **Isla de Ometepe,** which was formed by volcanoes, you will find prehistoric rock art. The Corn Islands are probably Nicaragua's most famous. They were once a haven for pirates— and now are a haven for tourists! If you're lucky, you can see sea turtles that come to nest on the Pacific beaches. You can even eat turtle eggs at many restaurants! Fishing is a very popular sport throughout the country, and as you can imagine, people eat a lot of seafood. Some other typical Nicaraguan foods are **gallo pinto, quesillos,** and **nacatamales.** Another important part of Nicaraguan culture is poetry. Rubén Darío is one of the country's best-known poets. You'll read a poem of his on the next page.

◎ ◎ ◎ ◎ ◎ Datos ◎ ◎ ◎ ◎ ◎

Capital: Managua

Ciudades importantes: León, Granada, Masaya, San Juan del Sur

Idiomas: Español y lenguas indígenas

Moneda: El córdoba

Población: 5.1 millones

¡Léelo en español!

Un poema de...
Rubén Darío Nicaragua
(1867–1916)

La princesa está triste... ¿Qué tendrá[1]
   la princesa?
Los suspiros[2] se escapan de su boca
   de fresa,
Que ha perdido[3] la risa, que ha
   perdido el color.
La princesa está pálida[4] en su silla
   de oro;
Está mudo el teclado[5] de su clave[6]
   sonoro,
Y en un vaso, olvidada se desmaya[7]
   una flor.

[1] what is the matter with   [2] sighs   [3] has lost
[4] pale   [5] keyboard   [6] harpsichord   [7] faints

Los tiburones del Lago Nicaragua
El Lago Nicaragua tiene otro nombre
de los indígenas—Cocibolca, lo que
significa "mar dulce." Es el lago más
grande de Centroamérica. El agua del
Lago Nicaragua es "agua dulce[1]."
Una sorpresa es que hay tiburones[2] en
el Lago Nicaragua. Es el único lugar
en todo el mundo donde los
tiburones viven en agua dulce. Los
científicos estudian estos tiburones.
El lago es tan[3] grande que hay más de
cuatrocientas islas. La isla más grande
se llama Isla de Ometepe. Es famosa
por sus estatuas y dibujos antiguos de
los indígenas chorotega.

[1] fresh water   [2] sharks   [3] so

Reading Strategy

Using Visuals What do you
know about sharks? Can you
find el **Lago Nicaragua** on a
map of Central America? What
do you notice about its location?
Use this information to help you
understand the reading.

Recognizing Cognates What
do you think these words mean:
sorpresa, científicos, estatuas?
Use these cognates to help you
understand what is being said
about Nicaragua.

¡Comprendo!

Answer in English.

1. List five things you learned about
   Nicaragua.

2. What is the largest lake in Central
   America?

3. What fish are found there? Why is
   this unusual?

Appendix

Nombres femeninos

Adela, Adelita Adele
Adriana Adrian, Adrienne
Alejandra Alexandra
Alicia Alice
Amalia Amelia
Ana Ann, Anna, Anne
Andrea Andrea
Ángela Angela
Anita Anita
Antonia Antonia

Bárbara Barbara
Beatriz Beatrice
Berta Bertha
Blanca Blanche

Carla Carla, Karla
Carlota Charlotte
Carmen Carmen
Carolina Caroline, Carolyn
Catalina Kathleen
Catarina Catherine, Kathryn
Cecilia Cecile
Clara Clara, Claire
Claudia Claudia
Constancia Constance
Consuelo Connie
Corina Corinne
Cristina Christine

Débora Deborah
Diana Diana, Diane
Dolores Dolores

Elena Ellen, Elaine, Helen
Elisa Lisa, Elise
Elsa Elsa
Ema Emma
Emilia Emily
Esperanza Hope
Estela Estelle, Stella
Ester Esther
Eugenia Eugenia
Eva Eve, Eva

Francisca Frances

Gabriela Gabrielle
Gloria Gloria
Gracia Grace
Graciela Grace

Inés Agnes, Inez
Irene, Irena Irene
Isabel Isabel, Elizabeth

Josefa Josephine, Josie
Josefina Josephine, Josie
Juana Jane, Jean, Joan
Judit Judith, Judy
Julia Julia

Laura Laura
Leonor Eleanor
Lidia Lydia
Linda Linda
Lola Lola
Lucía Lucy, Lucille
Lucinda Lucinda, Lucy
Luisa Louise, Lois

Margarita Margaret, Marguerite
María Mary, Maria, Marie
Mariana Mary Ann, Mariann
Marta Martha
Matilde Matilda
Mercedes Mercedes
Mónica Monica

Nora Nora, Norah

Olga Olga

Patricia Patricia
Paula Paula

Raquel Rachel
Rebeca Rebecca
Roberta Roberta
Rosa Rose
Rosalía Rosalie

Sara Sara, Sarah
Silvia Sylvia
Sofía Sophie
Sonia Sonia, Sonya
Susana Susan, Suzanne

Tania Tanya, Tania
Teresa Theresa, Therese
Toña Toni
Verónica Veronica
Victoria Victoria
Violeta Violet
Virginia Virginia

Nombres masculinos

Abrahán Abraham
Adán Adam
Agustín Augustine
Alberto Albert
Alejandro Alexander
Alfredo Alfred
Andrés Andrew
Ángel Angel
Antonio Anthony
Arnaldo Arnold
Arturo Arthur

Benito Benito
Benjamín Benjamin
Bernardo Bernard

Carlos Charles
Claudio Claude
Cristián Christian

Daniel Daniel
Darío Darryl
David David
Diego James
Domingo Dominick
Donaldo Donald

Edmundo Edmund
Eduardo Edward
Emilio Emil
Enrique Henry
Ernesto Ernest
Esteban Stephen, Steven
Eugenio Eugene

Fabián Fabian
Federico Frederick
Felipe Phillip
Francisco Francis

Gabriel Gabriel
Gerardo Gerard
Gilberto Gilbert
Gregorio Gregory
Guillermo William
Gustavo Gustaf, Gus

Heriberto Herbert
Hugo Hugo

Ignacio Ignatius

Jaime James
Javier Xavier
Jeremías Jeremy
Jorge George
José Joseph
Josué Joshua
Juan John
Juanito Jack, Johnny
Julián Julien
Julio Julius, Jules

León Leo, Leon
Leonardo Leonard
Lionel Lionel
Lorenzo Lawrence
Lucas Luke, Lucas
Luis Louis

Manuel Manuel, Emmanuel
Marcos Mark
Mario Mario
Martín Martin
Mateo Matthew, Matt
Mauricio Maurice
Miguel Michael, Mike

Nicolás Nicholas

Óscar Oscar

Pablo Paul
Paco, Pancho Frank
Patricio Patrick
Pedro Peter
Pepe Joey, Joe

Rafael Ralph
Raimundo Raymond
Ramón Raymond
Raúl Raoul
Ricardo Richard, Rick
Roberto Robert
Rodolfo Rudolph
Rogelio Roger
Rolando Roland
Rubén Ruben

Samuel Samuel
Saúl Saul
Simón Simon

Timoteo Timothy
Tomás Thomas, Tom

Vicente Vincent
Víctor Victor
Virgilio Virgil

Numbers

0	cero	34	treinta y cuatro	68	sesenta y ocho
1	uno	35	treinta y cinco	69	sesenta y nueve
2	dos	36	treinta y seis	70	setenta
3	tres	37	treinta y siete	71	setenta y uno
4	cuatro	38	treinta y ocho	72	setenta y dos
5	cinco	39	treinta y nueve	73	setenta y tres
6	seis	40	cuarenta	74	setenta y cuatro
7	siete	41	cuarenta y uno	75	setenta y cinco
8	ocho	42	cuarenta y dos	76	setenta y seis
9	nueve	43	cuarenta y tres	77	setenta y siete
10	diez	44	cuarenta y cuatro	78	setenta y ocho
11	once	45	cuarenta y cinco	79	setenta y nueve
12	doce	46	cuarenta y seis	80	ochenta
13	trece	47	cuarenta y siete	81	ochenta y uno
14	catorce	48	cuarenta y ocho	82	ochenta y dos
15	quince	49	cuarenta y nueve	83	ochenta y tres
16	dieciséis	50	cincuenta	84	ochenta y cuatro
17	diecisiete	51	cincuenta y uno	85	ochenta y cinco
18	dieciocho	52	cincuenta y dos	86	ochenta y seis
19	diecinueve	53	cincuenta y tres	87	ochenta y siete
20	veinte	54	cincuenta y cuatro	88	ochenta y ocho
21	veintiuno	55	cincuenta y cinco	89	ochenta y nueve
22	veintidós	56	cincuenta y seis	90	noventa
23	veintitrés	57	cincuenta y siete	91	noventa y uno
24	veinticuatro	58	cincuenta y ocho	92	noventa y dos
25	veinticinco	59	cincuenta y nueve	93	noventa y tres
26	veintiséis	60	sesenta	94	noventa y cuatro
27	veintisiete	61	sesenta y uno	95	noventa y cinco
28	veintiocho	62	sesenta y dos	96	noventa y seis
29	veintinueve	63	sesenta y tres	97	noventa y siete
30	treinta	64	sesenta y cuatro	98	noventa y ocho
31	treinta y uno	65	sesenta y cinco	99	noventa y nueve
32	treinta y dos	66	sesenta y seis	100	cien
33	treinta y tres	67	sesenta y siete		

Word List

Spanish-English

The Spanish-English Word List contains the Spanish words you learn in each unit, as well as words you come across in readings. A number in parentheses indicates the unit where a word was taught. (B) indicates the **¡Bienvenidos!** *(Welcome!)* unit.

Here's a sample entry—a word and its English equivalent:

la **computadora** computer (B)

The bold letters in different type tell you that **computadora** is the entry. "La" tells you to use "la," (not "el") with **computadora.** (B) tells you that **computadora** first appears in the **¡Bienvenidos!** unit.

Here's another entry:

¡Úsalo! *(com.; inf.: **usar**)* Use it! (B)

The abbreviations in parentheses—*com.* and *inf.*—tell you that **¡Úsalo!** is a command, and that it comes from the word **usar** ("to use").

Here are the complete Word List abbreviations:

Abbreviations

adj.	adjective	*inf.*	infinitive
adv.	adverb	*m.*	masculine
com.	command	*pl.*	plural
f.	feminine	*s.*	singular

A

a to (3), at (8)

  a las ocho at eight o'clock (8)

  ¿A qué hora? At what time? (8)

  a tiempo on time (8)

  a veces sometimes (6)

la **abanderada** (female) flag-bearer (1)

el **abanderado** (male) the flag-bearer (1)

  abril April (6)

la **abuela** grandmother (10)

el **abuelo** grandfather (10)

los **abuelos** grandparents (10)

  aburrido, aburrida boring (9)

  adiós good-bye (B)

  ¿Adónde? (to) where? (3)

    ¿Adónde vas? Where are you going? (4)

  agosto August (6)

  ahora now (5)

  al (*a + el*) to the (3)

  alto, alta tall (10)

la **alumna** (female) student (B)

el **alumno** (male) student (B)

los **amigos** (male or male and female) friends (B)

  amarillo, amarilla yellow (2)

  anaranjado, anaranjada orange (color) (2)

el **animal** (*pl.: animales*) animal (2)

  antipático, antipática unpleasant (10)

el **año** year (7)

  el Año Nuevo New Year (6)

  ¿Cuántos años tiene? How old is he/she? (7)

  los meses del año the months of the year (6)

  Tiene diez años. He/She is ten years old. (7)

  aprender to learn (9)

    aprender a to learn how to do something (9)

el **arte** art (4)

  así so (B)

    así, así so-so (B)

  ¡ay! oh!, ouch! (B)

  azul blue (2)

B

  bailar to dance (6)

  bajo, baja short (10)

  balón large ball (B)

la **bandera** flag (1)

  el Día de la Bandera Flag Day (6)

la **biblioteca** library (4)

  bien well, fine (B)

    Estoy bien. I'm fine (B)

    muy bien very well (4)

  ¡Bienvenidos! Welcome! (B)

la **bisabuela** great-grandmother (10)

el **bisabuelo** great-grandfather (10)

los **bisabuelos** great-grandparents (10)

  blanco, blanca white (2)

el **bolígrafo** ballpoint pen (1)

el **borrador** chalk eraser (1)

  buen good (*before a m. s. noun*) (5)

    Hace buen tiempo. The weather is nice. (5)

  bueno, buena good (B)

    ¡Buenas noches! Good evening!, Good night! (B)

    ¡Buenas tardes! Good afternoon! (B)

    ¡Buenos días! Good morning! (B)

C

el **calendario** calendar (3)

el **calor** heat (5)
    Hace calor. It's hot. (5)
    Tengo calor. I'm hot. (7)
  caminar to walk (6)

el **canario** canary (2)
  cantar to sing (4)

la **casa** house, home (3)
  celebrar to celebrate (6)

la **chica** girl (B)

el **chico** boy (B)

las **ciencias** science (9)

el **cine** movie theater, movies (3)
  ir al cine to go to the movies (3)

el **círculo** circle (2)
  claro of course (9)
  ¡Claro que sí! Of course! (1)

la **clase** class (4)
  el salón de clase classroom (1)

el **color** (pl.: *colores)* color (2)
  ¿De qué color es? What color
    is it? (2)
  ¿Cómo? How? (B) What?
    ¿Cómo es...? What is … like? (2)
    ¿Cómo estás? How are you
      (*familiar)*? (B)
    ¿Cómo se llama (el chico)?
      What's (the boy's) name? (B)
    ¿Cómo te llamas? What's your
      name? (*familiar)* (B)
  comprar to buy (6)
  comprender to understand (9)

la **computadora** computer (B)
  la clase de computadoras
    computer class (4)
  usar la computadora to use the
    computer (4)

el **conejo** rabbit (2)

la **conexión** connection (B)
  corto, corta short (2)

el **cuaderno** notebook (1)

el **cuadrado** square (2)
  ¿Cuál? ¿Cuáles? (*pl.)* Which
    one(s)? (5)
  ¿Cuál es tu número de teléfono?
    What's your phone number? (B)
  ¿Cuándo? When? (3)
  ¿Cuánto? ¿Cuánta? How much? (8)
    ¿Cuánto es... más...?
      What is… plus…? (B)
  ¿Cuántos? ¿Cuántas?
    How many? (B)
    ¿Cuántos/Cuántas... hay?
      How many... are there? (1)
    ¿Cuántos años tiene? How old
      is he/she? (7)

el **cuarto** quarter (8)
  un cuarto de hora a quarter of
    an hour (8)
  una hora y cuarto an hour and
    a quarter (8)

el **cumpleaños** birthday (6)
  ¿Cuándo es tu cumpleaños?
    When is your birthday? (6)

D

de of (1); in (8)
  de la mañana in the morning (8)
  de la tarde in the afternoon (8)
  ¿De qué color... ? What
    color… ? (2)

¿De quién? Whose? (10)

los **deportes** sports (4)

   practicar deportes to practice (play) sports (4)

el **día** day (3)

   ¡Buenos días! Good morning! (B)

   el Día de la Bandera Flag Day (6)

   el día de fiesta holiday (6)

   el Día de la Independencia Independence Day (6)

   el día de la semana weekday (3)

   dibujar to draw (6)

   diciembre December (6)

   difícil (*pl.: difíciles*) difficult (9)

   divertido, divertida amusing, entertaining, fun (9)

el **domingo** Sunday (3)

   los domingos on Sundays (3)

   ¿Dónde? Where? (3)

E

el **ecuador** equator (5)

la **educación física** physical education (9)

   el (*m. s.*) the (B)

   él he (6)

   ella she (6)

   en in, on (1)

   en punto on the dot, sharp (*time*) (8)

   enero January (6)

   entre between, among (B)

   entre amigos among friends (B)

   Es... It's... (B)

   escribir to write (9)

el **escritorio** large desk (B)

   escuchar to listen (4)

la **escuela** school (3)

el **español** Spanish (9)

   espectacular spectacular (9)

la **estación** season (5)

   estar to be (B)

   ¿Cómo está? How are you (*formal*)?

   ¿Cómo estás? How are you (*informal*)?

   Está lloviendo. It's raining. (5)

   Está nevando. It's snowing. (5)

   Está nublado. It's cloudy. (5)

   estás you are (*familiar*) (B)

   Estoy muy mal. I don't feel well at all. I'm not doing well. (B)

   estudiar to study (4)

los **estudios sociales** social studies (9)

F

   fabuloso(a) fabulous (9)

   fácil (*pl.: fáciles*) easy (9)

la **familia** family (10)

   fantástico, fantástica fantastic (9)

   favorito, favorita favorite (2)

   ¿Cuál es tu animal favorito? What's your favorite animal? (2)

   febrero February (6)

la **fecha** date (6)

   ¿Qué fecha es hoy? What's today's date? (6)

   feliz happy (6)

   ¡Feliz cumpleaños! Happy Birthday! (6)

   fin (*pl.: fines*) end (3)

   el fin de semana weekend (3)

   flaco, flaca thin (2)

el **flamenco** flamingo (2)

   fresco, fresca cool, fresh (5)

   Hace fresco. It's cool. (*weather*) (5)

   frío, fría cold (5)

   Hace frío. It's cold. (*weather*) (5)

   Tengo frío. I'm cold. (7)

G

el **gato**   cat (2)

el **gimnasio**   gymnasium (4)

el **globo**   globe (1)

gordo, gorda   fat (2)

gracias   thank you, thanks (B)

grande   big, large (2)

la **gripe**   flu (7)

   Tengo la gripe.   I have the flu. (7)

gris   gray (2)

guapo, guapa   good-looking (10)

gustar   to like (5)

   Le gusta el verano.   He/She likes summer. (5)

   Me gusta la primavera.   I like spring. (5)

   ¿Qué te gusta hacer?   What do you like to do? (6)

   ¿Te gusta pintar?   Do you like to paint? (5)

H

hablar   to talk (4)

hacer   to do (4)

   Hace calor.   It's hot. (5)

   Hace fresco.   It's cool. (5)

   Hace frío.   It's cold. (5)

   Hace sol.   It's sunny. (5)

   Hace viento.   It's windy. (5)

   ¿Qué tiempo hace?   What's the weather like? (5)

   ¿Qué vas a hacer?   What are you going to do? (4)

el **hambre** (*f.*)   hunger (7)

   ¡Tengo hambre!   I'm hungry! (7)

hasta   until (B)

   ¡Hasta luego!   See you later! (B)

   ¡Hasta mañana!   See you tomorrow! Until tomorrow! (B)

   ¡Hasta pronto!   See you soon! (B)

hay (*inf.: haber*)   there is, there are (1)

   ¿Cuántos... hay?   How many... are there? (1)

   ¿Qué hay...?   What is/are there...?

la **hermana**   sister (10)

la **hermanastra**   stepsister (10)

el **hermanastro**   stepbrother (10)

el **hermano**   brother (10)

los **hermanos**   brothers, brothers and sisters (10)

la **hija**   daughter (10)

el **hijo**   son (10)

los **hijos**   sons, children (10)

la **hoja de papel**   sheet of paper (1)

¡Hola!   Hello! Hi! (B)

el **hombre**   man (B)

la **hora**   hour (8)

   ¿A qué hora?   At what time? (8)

   media hora   a half-hour (8)

   ¿Qué hora es?   What time is it? (8)

   un cuarto de hora   a quarter of an hour (8)

   una hora y cuarto   an hour and a quarter (8)

   una hora y media   an hour and a half (8)

hoy   today (3)

   ¿Qué día es hoy?   What day is today? (3)

I

importante   important (9)

el **inglés**   English (9)

interesante   interesting (9)

el **invierno**   winter (5)

ir   to go (3)

   ¿Adónde vas?   Where are you going? (4)

   Voy a...   I'm going to... (4)

J

joven   young (10)

el **jueves**   Thursday (3)

   los jueves   on Thursdays

jugar   to play a game or sport (6)

julio   July (6)

junio   June (6)

L

la   *(f. s.)* the (B)

el **lápiz**   *(pl.: lápices)*   pencil (1)

largo, larga   long (2)

las   *(f. pl.)* the (1)

le   to him/her/you *(formal)* (5)

   le gusta   you *(formal)* like (5)

la **lección**   lesson (B)

la **lectura**   reading (9)

leer   to read (9)

el **libro**   book (1)

limpiar   to clean (6)

llamas   *(inf.: llamar)*   you call (B)

   Me llamo...   My name is... (B)

   Se llama...   His/Her name
      is... (B)

   Te llamas...   Your name is... (B)

Llueve.   *(inf.: llover)*   It's raining. (5)

el **loro**   parrot (2)

los   *(m. pl.)* the (1)

luego   later (B)

   ¡Hasta luego!   See you later! (B)

el **lunes**   Monday (3)

   los lunes   on Mondays (3)

la **luz** *(pl.: luces)*   light (B)

M

la **madrastra**   stepmother (10)

la **madre**   mother (10)

la **maestra**   (female) teacher (B)

el **maestro**   (male) teacher (B)

mal   *(adj., before a m. s. noun)* bad;
   (adv.) not well, badly (B)

   Estoy muy mal.   I don't feel well
      at all. I'm not doing well.   (B)

   Hace mal tiempo.   The weather
      is bad. (5)

la **mamá**   mother, mom (10)

mañana   *(adv.)* tomorrow (3)

   ¡Hasta mañana!   See you
      tomorrow! (B)

la **mañana**   morning (8)

   de la mañana   in the morning
      (a. m.) (8)

el **mapa**   map (1)

maravilloso, maravillosa
   wonderful (9)

el **marcador**   marker (1)

la **mariposa**   butterfly (2)

marrón   *(pl.: marrones)*   brown (2)

el **martes**   Tuesday (3)

   los martes   on Tuesdays

marzo   March (6)

más   plus (B)

   más o menos   so-so (B)

las **matemáticas**   mathematics (9)

mayo   May (6)

me   myself (B), to me (5)

   Me gusta...   I like... (5)

   Me llamo...   My name is... (B)

la **medianoche**   midnight (8)

medio, media   half (8)

   media hora   a half-hour   (8)

   una hora y media   an hour and
      a half (8)

el **mediodía**   noon, midday (8)

menos   to, of *(time)*   (8)

   Son las dos menos cuarto.
      It's fifteen to two. It's a quarter
      of two. (8)

el **mes** (*pl.: meses*) month (6)
la **mesa** table (1)
mi (*pl.: mis*) my (10)
el **miedo** fear (7)
   Tengo miedo. I'm scared. (7)
el **miércoles** Wednesday (3)
   los miércoles on Wednesdays (3)
el **minuto** minute (8)
morado, morada purple (2)
mucho (*adv.*) a lot (4)
la **mujer** (*pl.: mujeres*) woman (B)
la **música** music (4)
muy very (B)
   Muy bien, gracias. Very well, thanks. Very well, thank you. (B)

N

nadar to swim (6)
la **Navidad** Christmas (6)
negro, negra black (2)
nieva (*inf.: nevar*) It's snowing. (5)
la **nieta** granddaughter (10)
el **nieto** grandson (10)
los **nietos** grandchildren (10)
la **niña** girl (B)
el **niño** boy (B)
no no (1)
la **noche** night, evening (8)
   ¡Buenas noches! Good evening! Good night! (B)
noviembre November (6)
nublado (*adj.*) cloudy (5)
   Está nublado. It is cloudy. (5)
el **número** number (B)
   ¿Cuál es tu número de teléfono? What's your phone number? (B)
nunca never (6)

O

octubre October (6)
el **oso** bear (2)
el **otoño** autumn, fall (5)

P

el **padrastro** stepfather (10)
el **padre** father (10)
los **padres** fathers, parents (10)
el **pájaro** bird (2)
el **papá** father, dad (10)
los **papás** fathers, parents (10)
el **papel** paper (1)
   la hoja de papel sheet of paper (1)
la **papelera** wastebasket (1)
la **pared** (*pl.: paredes*) wall (1)
el **parque** park (3)
participar to participate (4)
patinar to skate (6)
pequeño, pequeña small, little (2)
el **perro** dog (2)
el **pez** (*pl.: peces*) fish (2)
pintar to paint (4)
el **pizarrón** chalkboard, blackboard, whiteboard (B)
por in (*time*) (8)
   por la mañana in the morning (8)
   por la noche in the evening (8)
   por la tarde in the afternoon (8)
   ¿Por qué? Why? (9)
   ¿Por qué no? Why not? (9)
practicar to practice (4)
practicar deportes to practice (play) sports (4)
la **prima** (female) cousin (10)

la **primavera** spring (5)

el **primero** the first (of the month) (3)

el **primo** (male) cousin (10)

los **primos** (male or male and female) cousins (10)

la **prisa** hurry (7)

    Tiene prisa. He/She is in a hurry. (7)

    pronto soon (B)

    ¡Hasta pronto! See you soon! (B)

    próximo, próxima next (3)

    la próxima semana next week (3)

la **puerta** door (B)

la **puesta del sol** sunset (8)

el **pupitre** (student's) desk (B)

Q

¿Qué? What? (B)

    ¿A qué hora? At what time? (8)

    ¿Qué es? What is it? (B)

    ¿Qué estación te gusta? Which season do you like? (5)

    ¿Qué hay ... ? What is/are there ... ? (1)

    ¿Qué hora es? What time is it? (8)

    ¿Qué número es? What number is it? (B)

    ¿Qué tal? How's it going? How are you doing? (B)

    ¿Qué te gusta hacer? What do you like to do? (6)

    ¿Qué tiempo hace? What's the weather like? (5)

    ¿Qué tienes? What's the matter? (7) What do you have? (1)

    ¿Qué vas a hacer? What are you going to do? (4)

¿Quién? ¿Quiénes? *(pl.)* Who? (B)

    ¿Quién es ...? Who is ...? (B)

    ¿Quiénes son? Who are they? (1)

R

el **ratón** (*pl.: ratones*) mouse (2)

la **raza** race (6)

    el Día de la Raza Columbus Day (6)

la **razón** (*pl.: razones*) reason (7)

    Tiene razón. He/She is right. (7)

el **rectángulo** rectangle (2)

la **regla** ruler (1)

el **reloj** (*pl.: relojes*) clock (1)

    rojo, roja red (2)

    rosado, rosada pink (2)

S

el **sábado** Saturday (3)

    los sábados on Saturdays (3)

la **salida del sol** sunrise (8)

el **salón de clase** classroom (1)

la **salud** health (9)

la **sed** thirst (7)

    Tengo sed. I'm thirsty (7)

    Se llama... His/her name is... (B)

la **semana** week (3)

    el día de la semana weekday (3)

    esta semana this week (3)

    el fin de semana weekend (3)

    la próxima semana next week (3)

    sensacional sensational (9)

    señor, Sr. Mister, Mr. (7)

el **señor** man, gentleman (7)

    señora, Sra. Mrs., ma'am (7)

la **señora** woman, lady (7)

    señorita, Srta. Miss (7)

la **señorita** young lady (7)

    septiembre September (6)

ser to be (B)

    ¿Qué es? What is it? (B)

    ¿Qué son? What are they? (1)

    ¿Quién es? Who is he/she? (B)

    ¿Quiénes son? Who are they? (1)

sí yes (1)

siempre always (6)

la **silla** chair (B)

simpático, simpática nice, friendly (10)

el **sol** sun (8)

    Hace sol. It's sunny. (5)

    la puesta del sol sunset (8)

    la salida del sol sunrise (8)

son (*inf.: ser*) they are (1)

su (*pl.: sus*) his, her, your (formal) (10)

el **sueño** sleep (7)

    Tengo sueño. I'm sleepy. (7)

la **suerte** luck (7)

    Tengo suerte. I'm lucky. (7)

T

también also, too (6)

tampoco neither, either (6)

la **tarde** afternoon, evening (8)

    ¡Buenas tardes! Good afternoon! Good evening! (B)

    por la tarde in the afternoon (p. m.) (8)

te yourself (B), to you (5)

    ¿Cómo te llamas? What's your name? (B)

    ¿Te gusta? Do you like it? (5)

el **teléfono** telephone (B)

    el número de teléfono telephone number (B)

tener to have (1), to be (7)

    ¿Qué tienes? What's the matter? What do you have? (7)

    tener... años to be... years old (7)

    tener calor to be hot (7)

    tener frío to be cold (7)

    tener la gripe to have the flu (7)

    tener hambre to be hungry (7)

    tener miedo to be scared (7)

    tener prisa to be in a hurry (7)

    tener razón to be right (7)

    tener sed to be thirsty (7)

    tener sueño to be sleepy (7)

    tener suerte to be lucky (7)

tengo (*inf.: tener*) I have (1)

terrible terrible (9)

la **tía** aunt (10)

el **tiempo** weather (5), time (8)

    a tiempo on time (8)

    Hace buen tiempo. The weather is nice. (5)

    Hace mal tiempo. The weather is bad. (5)

    ¿Qué tiempo hace? What's the weather like? (5)

la **tienda** store (3)

tienes (*inf.: tener*) you (*familiar*) have (1)

el **tigre** tiger (2)

el **tío** uncle (10)

los **tíos** uncles, aunts and uncles (10)

la **tiza** chalk (1)

trabajar to work (4)

el **triángulo** triangle (2)

tu (*pl.: tus*) your (*familiar*) (B)

tú you (*familiar*) (B)

U

un *(m.s.)* *(pl.: **unos**)* a, an (B)
una *(f.s.)* *(pl.: **unas**)* a, an (B)
la **unidad** *(pl.: **unidades**)* unit (1)
¡Úsalo! *(com., inf.: **usar**)* Use it! (B)
usar to use (4)
  usar la computadora to use the computer (4)
usted you *(formal)* (7)

V

va *(inf.: **ir**)* he/she goes/is going (3)
vas *(inf.: **ir**)* you *(familiar)* go/are going (3)
la **ventana** window (1)
el **verano** summer (5)
verde green (2)

vez time; occasion (6)
  a veces sometimes (6)
viejo, vieja old (10)
el **viento** wind (5)
  Hace viento. It's windy. (5)
el **viernes** Friday (3)
  los viernes on Fridays (3)
voy *(inf.: **ir**)* I go, I'm going (3)

Y

y and (B)
  ¿Y tú? And you? (B)
yo I (4)

Word List

English-Spanish

This list gives the English translation of Spanish words that you've learned in *¡Hola!*. A number in parentheses or (B) indicates the unit where a word is taught.

A

a, an un, una (B)
a lot mucho (4)
afternoon la tarde (8)
also también (6)
always siempre (6)
among friends entre amigos (B)
amusing divertido, divertida (9)
and y (B)
animal el animal (2)
April abril (6)
art el arte (4)
at a (8)
August agosto (6)
aunt la tía (10)
aunts and uncles los tíos (10)
autumn el otoño (5)

B

bad mal *(adj. before a m. s. noun)* (B)
badly mal *(adv.)* (B)
ball (large) balón (B)
ballpoint pen el bolígrafo (1)
to **be** ser, estar (B); tener (7)
 to be called llamarse (B)

to be cold tener frío (7)
to be hot tener calor (7)
to be hungry tener hambre (7)
to be in a hurry tener prisz (7)
to be going to ir a *(+ inf)* (4)
to be lucky tener suerte (7)
to be scared tener miedo (7)
to be sleepy tener sueño (7)
to be thirsty tener sed (7)
to be... years old tener... años (7)
bear el oso (2)
between friends entre amigos (B)
big grande (2)
bird el pájaro (2)
birthday el cumpleaños (6)
 Happy Birthday! ¡Feliz Cumpleaños! (6)
 When is your birthday? ¿Cuándo es tu cumpleaños? (6)
black negro, negra (2)
blackboard el pizarrón (B)
blue azul (2)
book el libro (1)
boring aburrido, aburrida (9)
boy el chico, el niño (B)
brother el hermano (10)

brothers and sisters
   los hermanos (10)
brown   marrón (2)
butterfly   la mariposa (2)
to **buy**   comprar (6)

C

calendar   el calendario (3)
canary   el canario (2)
cat   el gato (2)
to **celebrate**   celebrar (6)
chair   la silla (B)
chalk   la tiza (1)
chalkboard   el pizarrón (B)
chalk eraser   el borrador (1)
children   los hijos (10)
circle   el círculo (2)
class   la clase (1)
classroom   el salón de clase (1)
to **clean**   limpiar (6)
clock   el reloj (1)
cold   frío, fría (5)
   I'm cold.   Tengo frío. (7)
color   el color (2)
computer   la computadora (B)
connection   la conexión (B)
cool   fresco, fresca (5)
cousin (female)   la prima (10)
cousin (male)   el primo (10)
cousins   los primos (10)

D

dad   el papá (10)
to **dance**   bailar (6)
date   la fecha (6)
   What's today's date?   ¿Qué fecha
      es hoy? (6)

daughter   la hija (10)
day   el día (3)
December   diciembre (6)
desk (student's)   el pupitre (B)
desk (office)   el escritorio (B)
difficult   difícil (*pl.: difíciles*) (9)
to **do**   hacer (4)
dog   el perro (2)
door   la puerta (B)
to **draw**   dibujar (6)

E

easy   fácil (*pl.: fáciles*) (9)
either   tampoco (6)
English   el inglés (9)
equator   el ecuador (5)
end   el fin (*pl. fines*) (3)
entertaining   divertido, divertida
eraser (chalk)   el borrador (1)
evening   la tarde, la noche (8)

F

fall   el otoño (5)
fantastic   fantástico, fantástica (9)
fat   gordo, gorda (2)
father   el papá, el padre (10)
favorite   favorito, favorita (2)
fear   el miedo (7)
February   febrero (6)
few, a   unos, unas (2)
fine   bien (B)
first, the (*of the month*)
   el primero (3)
fish   el pez (*pl.: peces*) (2)
flag   la bandera (1)
flag bearer   el abanderado, la
   abanderada

Flag Day el Día de la bandera
flamingo el flamenco (2)
flu gripe (7)
   I have the flu. Tengo la gripe. (7)
Friday viernes (3)
   on Fridays los viernes (3)
friendly simpático, simpática (10)
friends amigos (B)
fun divertido, divertida (9)

G

gentleman el señor (7)
girl la chica, la niña (B)
globe el globo (1)
to **go** ir (3)
   to be going to (+ *inf.*) ir a
     (+ *inf.*) (4)
good buen (*before a m. s. noun*) (5),
   bueno, buena (B)
Good afternoon. Buenas tardes. (B)
good-bye adiós (B)
Good evening. Buenas noches. (B)
good-looking guapo, guapa (10)
Good morning. Buenos días. (B)
Good night. Buenas noches. (B)
grandchildren los nietos (10)
granddaughter la nieta (10)
grandfather el abuelo (10)
grandmother la abuela (10)
grandparents los abuelos (10)
grandson el nieto (10)
gray gris (2)
great-grandfather el bisabuelo (10)
great-grandmother la bisabuela (10)
great-grandparents
   los bisabuelos (10)
green verde (2)
gymnasium el gimnasio (4)

H

half medio, media (8)
half-hour media hora (8)
Happy Birthday!
   ¡Feliz cumpleaños! (6)
to **have** tener (1)
he él (6)
health la salud (9)
Hello! ¡Hola! (B)
her su (*pl.: sus*) (10)
Hi! ¡Hola! (B)
his su (*pl.: sus*) (10)
home la casa (3)
hot calor
   I'm hot. Tengo calor. (7)
   It's hot. Hace calor. (5)
hour la hora (8)
   an hour and a half una hora
     y media (8)
   an hour and a quarter una hora
     y cuarto (8)
house la casa (3)
How? ¿Cómo? (B)
   How are you? ¿Cómo estás?
     (*familiar*)
   How are you doing? How's it
     going? ¿Qué tal? (B)
   How many? ¿Cuántos...?
     ¿Cuántas...? (B)
   How many... are there?
     Cuántos/Cuántas... hay? (1)
   How much? ¿Cuánto?
     ¿Cuánta? (8)
   How old is he/she? ¿Cuántos años
     tiene? (7)
hungry: **I'm hungry!** ¡Tengo
   hambre! (7)
hurry la prisa (7)
   He/She is in a hurry.
     Tiene prisa. (7)

I

I yo (4)

I'm not doing well. Estoy muy mal. (B)

I'm scared. Tengo miedo. (7)

I feel very bad. / I don't feel well at all. Estoy muy mal. (B)

important importante (9)

in en (1), de (8)

  in the afternoon de la tarde, por la tarde (8)

  in the evening de la noche, por la noche (8)

  in the morning de la mañana, por la mañana (8)

interesting interesante (9)

It's... Es… (B) Está… (5)

  It's cloudy. Está nublado. (5)

  It's cold. Hace frío. (5)

  It's cool. Hace fresco. (5)

  It's hot. Hace calor. (5)

  It's raining. Está lloviendo. Llueve. (5)

  It's snowing. Está nevando. Nieva. (5)

  It's sunny. Hace sol. (5)

  It's windy. Hace viento. (5)

J

January enero (6)

July julio (6)

June junio (6)

K

to **know** saber (B)

  Do you know...? ¿Sabes que…? (B)

  Did you know...? ¿Sabías que…? (B)

L

lady la señora (7)

  young lady la señorita (7)

large grande (2)

to **learn** aprender (9)

  to learn how to do something aprender a (9)

library la biblioteca (4)

light la luz (B)

to **like** gustar (5)

  Do you like to paint? ¿Te gusta pintar? (5)

  He/She likes summer. Le gusta el verano. (5)

  I like spring. Me gusta la primavera. (5)

  What do you like to do? ¿Qué te gusta hacer? (6)

to **listen** escuchar (4)

little pequeño, pequeña (2)

long largo, larga (2)

lucky: I'm lucky Tengo suerte. (7)

M

man el hombre (B)

map el mapa (1)

March marzo (6)

marker el marcador (1)

marvelous maravilloso, maravillosa (9)

mathematics las matemáticas (9)

May mayo (6)

midday el mediodía (8)

midnight la medianoche (8)

minute el minuto (8)

Miss Señorita, Srta. (B)

mom la mamá, la madre (10)

Monday lunes (3)

  on Mondays los lunes (3)

month el mes (6)

morning la mañana (8)
  Good morning! ¡Buenos días!
  in the morning de la mañana/por la mañana (8)
mother la madre, la mamá (10)
mouse el ratón (*pl.: ratones*) (2)
movie theater el cine (3)
movies el cine (3)
  to go to the movies ir al cine (3)
music la música (4)
Mr. Señor, Sr. (7)
Mrs. Señora, Sra. (7)
my mi (*s.*), mis (*pl.*) (10)
  My name is... Me llamo… (B)

N

neither tampoco (6)
never nunca (6)
New Year el Año Nuevo (6)
next próximo, próxima (3)
nice simpático, simpática (10)
night la noche (8)
  Good night! ¡Buenas noches! (B)
no no
noon el mediodía (8)
not no (1)
notebook el cuaderno (1)
November noviembre (6)
now ahora (5)
number el número (B)

O

October octubre (6)
of de (1)
  Of course! ¡claro! ¡claro que sí! (9)
oh! ¡ay! (B)
old viejo, vieja (10)
on en (1)
  on time a tiempo (8)

orange (color) anaranjado, anaranjada (2)
ouch! ¡ay! (8)

P

to **paint** pintar (4)
paper (sheet of) (la hoja de) papel (1)
parents los papás, los padres (10)
park el parque (3)
parrot el loro (2)
to **participate** participar (4)
pen (ballpoint) el bolígrafo (1)
pencil el lápiz (*pl.: lápices*) (1)
physical education la educación física (9)
pink rosado, rosada (2)
to **play** jugar (6)
to **play sports** practicar deportes (4)
plus más (B)
purple morado, morada (2)

Q

quarter of an hour un cuarto de hora (8)

R

rabbit el conejo (2)
to **read** leer (9)
reading la lectura (9)
rectangle el rectángulo (2)
red rojo, roja (2)
right, to be tener razón (7)
ruler la regla (1)

S

Saturday sábado (3)
  on Saturdays los sábados
school la escuela (3)
science las ciencias (9)
season la estación
  (*pl.: estaciones*) (5)
See you later! ¡Hasta luego! (B)
See you soon! ¡Hasta pronto! (B)
See you tomorrow! ¡Hasta
  mañana! (B)
sensational sensacional
  (*pl.: sensacionales*) (9)
September septiembre (6)
sheet of paper la hoja de papel (1)
short corto, corta (2), bajo, baja (10)
to **sing** cantar (4)
sister la hermana (10)
to **skate** patinar (6)
sleepy: **I'm sleepy.** Tengo sueño. (7)
small pequeño, pequeña (2)
snowing nevar (5)
  It's snowing. Está nevando.
    Nieva. (5)
social studies los estudios
  sociales (9)
some unos, unas (2)
sometimes a veces (6)
son el hijo (10)
soon pronto (7)
  See you soon! ¡Hasta pronto! (B)
so-so así, así; más o menos (B)
Spanish el español (9)
sports los deportes (4)
  to play sports practicar
    deportes (4)
spring la primavera (5)
square el cuadrado (2)
stepbrother el hermanastro (10)
stepfather el padrastro (10)
stepmother la madrastra (10)

stepsister la hermanastra (10)
store la tienda (3)
student (female) la alumna (B)
student (male) el alumno (B)
student's desk el pupitre (B)
to **study** estudiar (4)
summer el verano (5)
sun el sol (8)
Sunday domingo (3)
  on Sundays los domingos (3)
sunrise la salida del sol (8)
sunset la puesta del sol (8)
to **swim** nadar (6)

T

table la mesa (1)
to **talk** hablar (4)
tall alto, alta (10)
teacher (male) el maestro,
  (female) la maestra (B)
telephone el teléfono (B)
telephone number el número de
  teléfono (B)
terrible terrible (9)
thank you gracias (B)
thanks gracias (B)
the el (*m. s.*), la (*f. s.*), los (*m. pl.*), las
  (*f. pl.*) (B)
there is/ there are hay (1)
thin flaco, flaca (2)
thirsty: **I'm thirsty.** Tengo sed. (7)
this week esta semana (3)
Thursday jueves (3)
  on Thursdays los jueves (3)
tiger el tigre (2)
time el tiempo, la hora (8)
to a (4)
to the (*m. s.*) al (3)
  to go to the movies ir al cine (3)

today   hoy (3)

  What day is today?   ¿Qué día es hoy? (3)

tomorrow   mañana (3)

  See you tomorrow!   ¡Hasta mañana! (B)

too   también (6)

triangle   el triángulo (2)

Tuesday   martes (3)

  on Tuesdays   los martes (3)

U

uncle   el tío (10)

to **understand**   comprender (9)

unit   la unidad (*pl.: unidades*) (1)

unpleasant   antipático, antipática (10)

until   hasta (B)

to **use**   usar (4)

  to use the computer   usar la computadora (4)

V

very   muy (B)

W

to **walk**   caminar (6)

wall   la pared (*pl.: paredes*) (1)

wastebasket   la papelera (1)

weather   el tiempo (5)

  The weather is nice.   Hace buen tiempo. (5)

  The weather is bad.   Hace mal tiempo. (5)

  What's the weather like?   ¿Qué tiempo hace? (5)

Wednesday   miércoles (3)

  on Wednesdays   los miércoles (3)

week   la semana (3)

weekday   el día de la semana (3)

weekend   el fin de semana (3)

Welcome!   ¡Bienvenidos! (B)

well   bien (B)

  Very well, thanks/thank you.   Muy bien, gracias. (B)

What?   ¿Qué? (B); ¿Cómo? (B)

  At what time?   ¿A qué hora? (8)

  What are you going to do?   ¿Qué vas a hacer? (4)

  What color is it?   ¿De qué color es? (2)

  What do you have?   ¿Qué tienes? (7)

  What do you like to do?   ¿Qué te gusta hacer? (6)

  What is it?   ¿Qué es? (B)

  What is... plus... ?   ¿Cuánto es... más... ? (B)

  What's (the boy's) name?   ¿Cómo se llama (el chico)? (B)

  What's the matter?   ¿Qué tienes? (1)

  What's the weather like?   ¿Qué tiempo hace? (5)

  What's your favorite animal?   ¿Cuál es tu animal favorito? (2)

  What's your name?   ¿Cómo te llamas? (B)

  What's your phone number?   ¿Cuál es tu número de teléfono? (B)

  What number is it?   ¿Qué número es? (B)

  What time is it?   ¿Qué hora es? (8)

When?   ¿Cuándo? (3)

Where (to)? ¿Dónde? ¿Adónde? (3)
  Where are you going? ¿Adónde vas? (4)
Which? ¿Cuál? (*pl.: ¿Cuáles?*) (5)
  What season do you like? ¿Qué estación te gusta? (5)
white blanco, blanca (2)
Who? ¿Quién? (B)
  Who is...?
    ¿Quién es…? (B)
Whose? ¿De quién? (10)
Why? ¿Por qué? (9)
windy: It's windy. Hace viento. (5)
window la ventana (1)
winter el invierno (5)
woman la mujer (B)
women las mujeres (B)
to **work** trabajar (4)
to **write** escribir (9)

Y

year el año (7)
  He / She is ten years old. Tiene diez años. (7)
yellow amarillo, amarilla (2)
yes sí (1)
you tú (*familiar*) (B), usted (*formal*) (*pl.: ustedes*) (7)
young joven (10)
  young lady la señorita (7)
your tu (*familiar*) (*pl.: tus*) (B); su (*formal*) (*pl.: sus*) (10)

Index

Acknowledgments

Photo Credits: © AFP/Corbis, p. 244 top right; © Tony Arruza/Corbis, p. 137; © Nigel Atherton/Stone/Getty Images, p. 71 bottom; © Bill Bachmann/Painet, p. 103 bottom; © Bill Bachmann/Photo Researcher's Inc., p. 139 left inset; © Bettmann/Corbis, pp. 72-73 spread, 224 bottom; © Steve Bly/Image Bank/Getty Images, p. 85; © Tibor Bognar/Corbis, p. 203 right; © Francis Caldwell/Painet, p. 25 top left; © Stephanie Cardinale/Corbis, p. 244 top center; © Myrleen Ferguson Cate/Photo Edit Inc., pp. 2-3 spread; © Bruce Clarke/Index Stock Imagery, p. 247 bottom; © Chris Collins/Corbis, p. 133 #5b; © Corbis, pp. 27, 81 top right, #1, #3, 133 #6b; © Sylvia Cordaiy/Photographers Direct, p. 130 bottom right; © J.P. Courau/DDBstock, 205 top; © Mary Kate Denny/Photo Edit Inc., p. 16 bottom left, 73 top; © Steve Dunwell/Index Stock Imagery, p. 130 top left; © Michael Fogden/Animals Animals, p. 54; © Rufus F. Folkks/Corbis, p. 244 top left; © Owen Franken/Corbis, p. 120; © Getty Images, pp. 45 top, 46-47 spread; 47 top right, 59, 62 top left, bottom left, top right, 68, 81 #2, 86 bottom left, 93 bottom, 117 bottom, 124, 130 top right, 133 top, #1a, #2a, #3a, #3b, #6a, 134, 158 inset, 181, 244 insets, 247 top; © Tony Freeman/PhotoEdit Inc., pp. 95 left, 176; © Robert Frerck/Odyssey Productions, p. 133 #4b; © Ned Gillette/Gillette Photography, p. 117 top
left; © Russell Gorden/Danita Delimont, p. 97; © Ken Graham/Stone/Getty Images, p. 133 #2b; © Spencer Grant/PhotoEdit Inc., pp. 14 #1, 16 bottom right, 161 right, 227 bottom; © Jeff Greenberg/Photo Edit Inc., p. 81 #4; © H. Huntly Hersch/DDBstock, p. 9 bottom; © Kit Houghton/Corbis, p. 203 left; © Dave G. Houser/Corbis, p. 159 top; © Wolfgang Kaehler, pp. 25 bottom right, 227 right; © Jerry Koontz/Index Stock Imagery, p. 234 bottom right; © Bob Krist/AGPix.com, pp. 116-117 spread, 139 right inset; © Claudia Kunin/Corbis, p. 16 top right; © Suzanne Murphy-Larronde/DDBstock, p. 71 top; © Suzanne Murphy-Larronde, 159 top; © Suzanne Murphy-Larronde/PhotNetworkStock, p. 82; © MarkLewis/Stone/Getty Images, p. 14 top right; © Richard Levine/Photographer's Direct, p. 224 inset; © Craig Lowell/Corbis, p. 47 bottom left; © Larry Luxner, pp. 33, 160-161 spread; 183 ; © Dennis MacDonald/PhotoEdit Inc., pp. 138-139 spread, 147; © Don Mason/Corbis, p. 133 #5a; © Chris Mattison; Frank Lane Picture Agency/Corbis, p. 67; © Merrill Images/Danita Delimont, p. 226-227 spread; © Lawrence Migdale, pp. 14 #2, #4, 159 bottom, 159 bottom; © Andres Morya /AGPix.com, p. 182-183 spread; © MichaeNewman/PhotoEdit Inc., p. 234 bottom left, top left, top right, © Rueters Newmedia Inc., pp. 224 top, 244 bottom center; © Erwin Nielsen/Painet, p. 183 top right; © Frank Nowakowski, pp. 161 bottom left, 161 right; © Carlos Pereyra/DDBstock, p. 95 top; © Helene Rogers/Art Directors, p. 3 inset top right; © Kevin Schafer/Corbis, pp.115, 138; © Premium Stock/Corbis, p. 45 bottom; © Laura Sivell/Corbis, p. 133 #1b; 125; © Ricardo Carrasco Stuparich, pp. 3 inset, 94-95 spread, 204-205 spread; © Keren Su/Taxi/Getty Images, p. 62 top right; © Art Wolfe/Image Bank/Getty Images, p. 55; © Yellow Dog Productions/Image Bank/Getty, Images, p. 14 #3; © Nevada Wier/Corbis, p. 130 bottom left.